The

JEFFERSON'S

of

WHITEHAVEN

The

JEFFERSON'S

of

WHITEHAVEN

TRADE **RJH** MARK

by

Brian Parnaby

Published by: Travail Press
              Marron Farm
              Ullock
              Cumbria
              CA14 4TP

ISBN: 978-0-9551716-0-4

Printed in Great Britain by Athenaeum Press Ltd.

The Jefferson Family
of Whitehaven

Preface

To assist the Reader and in view of possible confusion which may be caused by the repetitive Jefferson Family Christian names such as Robert and Henry (and also for simplicity of comprehension) I have made the following adjustments to the text:

Where the names Henry and Robert refer to different generations I have inserted the figures (1), (2), etc. after each forename, in order to identify which particular character is referred to in the narrative.

Additionally, I have included in the book separate personal histories of the main characters, each one designated with its appropriate generation hierarchical number, (1), (2) etc. This may mean some cross-referencing but should not deflect the reader from the text. I have also included a rather lengthy form of 'Family Tree' which endeavours, not perhaps totally successfully, to simplify the identification of the successive generations.

*To simplify matters for the Reader it may well
be advisable to ignore all the suffixes (1).(2), (3)
etc. and consider only that a 'Robert' or a
'Henry' Jefferson is involved, regardless of
generation.*

*Unfortunately, the remaining members of the
Jefferson family have been unable to produce
any photographs or illustrations of the family
members, these apparently having been lost over
the years. This includes photographs of the
various family dwellings. As partial
compensation I have included in the List of
Illustrations whatever copies of illustrations,
engravings, etc. I have been able to trace
through the family archives held in the Record
Offices and various other establishments.*

*No information on the family Estates in Antigua
is available through Archive material. Some,
however, is contained in 'The Rum Centre'
attraction in Whitehaven – well worth a visit as
it is of great historical interest and not just as
regards the Jefferson family interests. I have
endeavoured to obtain as much information as
possible direct from source – the Antigua &
Barbuda Archives – and the reader can judge
for him/her self how successful I have been. In
my opinion, one of the reasons for the present
day lack of Estate details, if not the main
reason, is that, at the time of the conveyancing
from the previous owners in Antigua, to the*

*Jefferson family, there were Four Hundred
Slaves employed on the Yeaman Estate.
Consequently in this advanced and sophisticated
age of the Twenty-First Century, these are four
hundred reasons for not placing this
embarrassing fact in the public domain. To the
great credit of the new owners, Jefferson's,
these slaves were emancipated as soon as
ownership passed into their hands. At no time
were any slaves shipped from the West Indies to
England in any Vessels, owned or chartered by
the Jefferson's. Consequently, there is no
shame to be cast on the family. In any case,
matters of historical fact should not be 'glossed'
over for reasons of sensitivity or political
correctness. What has happened cannot be
altered.*

*The reader must be assured that any views
expressed or implied in this book are the
personal opinions of the Author only and are
not necessarily factually and historically
correct.*

Acknowledgements

My main thanks are due to Ms Barbara Clark, of the Archive Service, Cumbria Record Office, Carlisle, for permission to use her dissertation on the 'Jefferson family of Whitehaven' for purposes of research.

I have also received kind help from the Staff at the Cumbria County Record Office at Whitehaven for which I am most grateful.

As regards the Jefferson's Shipping Fleet, I consulted that most excellent book 'From Cumberland to Cape Horn', by Dave Hollett. For anyone interested in the History of Whitehaven as a major shipbuilding town, or for students of Whitehaven history, generally, I heartily recommend this publication.

Unfortunately, when visiting the Garden of Rest on the site of the long demolished Holy Trinity Church, in Scotch Street, Whitehaven, I was unable to decipher any 'Jefferson' names on those headstones in the Garden. However, with the aid of various Church Histories in Whitehaven Library, I was able to obtain some names and dates of Burials, in both Holy Trinity and St. Nicholas's Churchyards and have included them in the Jefferson family history.

Information on the Jefferson's Antiguan business enterprises was rather harder to find and what I have obtained came mainly from 'The Rum Story' Exhibition in Whitehaven – an attraction well worth more than one visit – and also from a source in London - the High Commission for Antigua and Barbuda - and, in the West Indies, from the British High Commission in St John's Antigua and the Director, Antigua and Barbuda Archives, St. John's, Antigua.

I am grateful also to Mr Terry Ponting, Chief Executive of The Whitehaven Development Company, for providing me with a colour slide taken of a painting of Jefferson's Brigantine 'British Queen' which I have included in the illustrations to this book.

Past Editions of the Whitehaven News provided me with some personal information on those members of the Jefferson family who served in the old Westmorland and Cumberland Yeomanry. There is also reference to a member of the Jefferson family in a very informative book by Colin Bardgett,, on the formation and history of the Westmorland and Cumberland Yeomanry. For students of local military history this is a most interesting read as local family names predominate.

My thanks also to Ms Elizabeth Jefferson, who gave approval for the writing of this book and also for pointing me in the right direction when I was seeking information or clarification on certain matters.

Acknowledgement is also due to the late Daniel Hay, Librarian and Author. He was mainly responsible for placing the town of Whitehaven firmly on the map, as regards its historical past. His enthusiasm for his adopted town was remarkable and his scholarship exceptional.

The

JEFFERSON'S

of

WHITEHAVEN

INDEX TO CHAPTERS

APPENDICES

CHAPTER
I

The birth of a Dynasty

*Robert Jefferson**

**(*Robert (1) the first Robert, from
which the dynasty was to spring)**

Born:	*January 1704*
Died:	*18th October 1779*

The Founder of the dynasty was born at Aikton, near Wigton, Cumberland (now Cumbria) in 1704 and was baptised in the local Church on 19th January 1704. The Jefferson family had owned land in that area since the late Seventeenth century.

*On reaching adulthood he moved to Whitehaven where he became a **Master Mariner**. Whitehaven, then being one of the most important and prosperous ports in the Country made his choice of profession quite understandable.*

*At that time, the early eighteenth century, there was significant overseas trade between England and the Americas and Robert became involved in trade between Whitehaven and Virginia. He did not at that time own his own vessel but sailed as Master on chartered ships. The principal cargo was **tobacco**, a most lucrative business as there was a strong national demand for this product.*

This trade had been started over a half-century earlier at the instigation of Sir John Lowther, a major Landowner and redoubtable businessman. A considerable number of vessels were employed in this same trade, sailing from Whitehaven; some reports quoting the number as upwards of fifty vessels.

Most sea captains of that area, as well as commanding their ships, participated in trade such as this. The ships outward bound from Whitehaven always carried goods needed at their destinations and did not travel just in ballast. Coal was one of the principal cargoes exported, not only to Dublin but also to Virginia, Whitehaven coal being recognised as of the highest quality. Robert made purchases for export of a diverse range of products and from a variety of sources, as far afield as South-West Scotland and the Isle of Man. These he exported in his capacity as a Merchant Mariner and, at that time, it was an extremely profitable trade. Merchants such as Robert plying this two-way trade made double-profits on their ventures, despite the competition, there being such a high demand in England for their imports of tobacco, wines, spirits and other commodities.

Robert married Martha Skelton of Whitehaven in 1746 at the age of 42, quite old in that era of relatively short life spans. This marriage took place at the old Holy Trinity Church in Scotch Street, Whitehaven. This Church, now sadly demolished, was to play an important part in the lives of the Jefferson family, being the scene of baptisms, weddings and funerals over several generations. Inspection of the grounds in recent times have failed to reveal any Headstones belonging to the Jefferson family, all these having been uprooted when the Church grounds were converted into a Garden of Rest a few years ago. Additionally, the weather has played an important part in disfiguring those Headstones still on display. Many were made of the local St. Bees Sandstone and much of the lettering and inscriptions has become eroded through the action of wind and rain. For those who may be interested in pursuing their hobby of scrutinising Headstones, information in the bibliography at the end of this book will be of assistance. Those Headstones still on display have been placed against the rear walls surrounding the Churchyard or flat on the ground in an area set aside for that purpose. Disfigurement by moss and earth makes it difficult to decipher many names but some cleaning may reveal a little more detail.

Following their marriage, Robert and Martha lived in Marlborough Street where they raised their family. It would appear that they spent all their married life at that address. Robert, being a seafarer would find the location very convenient as the street is immediately adjacent to the Harbour and but a few steps away from the hub of activity of the port.

The couple had eight children, not an unusually large family in those days. The first born was Thomas, in 1749, who was baptised in Holy Trinity Church. He lived for 21 years but died in 1770 and was interred in Holy Trinity Churchyard, Lowther Street, Whitehaven (not in St. Nicholas's Churchyard as was previously thought.) The second child, Henry (1) was born in 1750 and was to become the actual Founder of the family business. Another son, Robert* was born in 1752 and died in New York in 1783 at the age of thirty-one years. Several other children followed over the next seven years but experienced only short lives. These were John (born 1757, died at nine months); Daniel (born 1758, died at four weeks); Mary (born 1759, died 1762, at age of three years). Another child, also named Mary was born in 1764 and died, unmarried, in 1787, at the age of twenty three years. Church records show that when Thomas *was interred in Holy Trinity Churchyard, he was placed with 'three infants lying near him'). In all likelihood these were the bodies of John, Daniel and the 'first' Mary.*

There is an anomaly in the notification of births however. Recorded in the Registers of the Holy Trinity Church is the name of a female, born in 1754 and baptised as 'Sarah', daughter of Robert and Martha (Jefferson). Sarah is not mentioned in other Jefferson records and there is therefore some doubt as to whether she was the child of Robert and Martha, there being other 'Jefferson' families living in the Whitehaven area during those years. Marriage Records of Holy Trinity Church show that one Sarah Jefferson married William Bacon, a Mariner, in 1780. If that was the same Sarah, then the age is right as she would have been twenty-six. However, none of the witnesses to the marriage belonged to the Jefferson family. There is also no record of a Sarah Jefferson amongst the Jefferson family papers as having died in infancy.

Robert's second eldest son, Henry (1) joined his Father in the Shipping trade in about 1775 (the eldest son Thomas had died in 1770), and for some years they were jointly involved in that business, predominantly between Whitehaven and Virginia. In 1775 the Jefferson's acquired their first ship, jointly owned by Robert and Henry. This was the 'Gale' a 'Snow' (Brig) of 200 tons,

Henry becoming its Master. The 'Gale' launched in 1758, had been named after the well-known Whitehaven family of Merchants. The 'Gale' made several voyages for the Jefferson's under Henry (1) before being sold in 1781.

The Jefferson Wine and Spirit Merchants' business was founded in the eighteenth century (in 1785), after Robert's death; Henry (1) being the actual Founder and not Robert who had died five years before.

Robert died in on 18th October 1779 at his Marlborough Street home, so it can be presumed that he lived for all his married life at that address. He lies buried in the Churchyard at Holy Trinity. The appearance of Marlborough Street has drastically altered since the halcyon days of the local 'Merchant Princes'. From the late Nineteenth century the grand houses gradually fell into disrepair and squalor, the area becoming more or less a slum and a blot on the landscape of Whitehaven, a beautiful Georgian Town. After the Second World War slum clearance work was effected; buildings in Marlborough and adjacent Streets were demolished and the inhabitants relocated to new Housing Estates on the fringes of the town.

Robert's obituary in the 'Cumberland Pacquet' in 1779 paid compliment to his status in the town. He was described as ' ....for many years a

captain in a ship in the Virginia trade...........
and........ much respected as an honest man'.

(* not included in the numbering as he was never involved in the family business, not locally anyway.)

CHAPTER
II

The Founder of the Firm

*Henry Jefferson**

**(*Henry (1) the first Henry, Founder of the
Family Business – son of Robert** *(Chapter I)*

Born : *1750*
Died : *1827*

*Like his Father, Henry began his working life as
a **Mariner**, becoming **Master** of the Snow, **Gale**,
a 200 ton vessel, plying the 'Atlantic Trade'. The
Lloyd's Register of 1775 described the Vessel as
being built in Whitehaven with Henry Jefferson
as co-owner (with his Father, Robert (1)) and
Captain and involved in trade with Virginia. The
main cargo would be tobacco, for which there
was high demand in England. Henry followed
this trade for four years, until 1779, trading
between London, Quebec and Virginia.*

*Sometime during this period he had also begun
trading in the West Indies and had established
business and social contacts with families in
Antigua. On 18th May 1780, at St. John's,*

Antigua, he married Ann(e) Tweedie, the daughter of Robert Tweedie, a Planter, of that Island. Ann(e) had been born in 1766 and was therefore only fourteen years of age when she married Henry who was, by then, thirty years old.

They probably returned to England in 1786, as Robert had been born in Antigua in 1785 (and presumably also his elder sisters Anne and Jane). They settled in Whitehaven, at his home number 4 Cross Street. There, Ann(e) proceeded to give birth to a large number of children, at regular intervals, fourteen in all, between 1782 and 1803. The union between Henry and Ann(e) resulted in a generations-long association between the Jefferson family and the Islands of Antigua and neighbouring St.Kitt's. A more in depth report on the Jefferson family's business dealings in this area can be found in Chapters 9-11.

Henry and Ann(e)'s first child was Anne (born 1782). Then followed Jane (also in 1782?) and Robert (2) in 1785 (all born in Antigua). The remainder were apparently born in Whitehaven, following the family's return from Antigua. Sarah (1787); Mary (date of birth not known); Harriet (1791); Sarah (also in 1791); Elizabeth (1793); Eleanor (1795); Catherine (1797); Charlotte (1800); Henry (2) (also 1800); Margaret (1801) and Thomas (1803). Apparently, all these children were baptised at Holy Trinity Church.

The longevity of the children of their union was varied. Of the fourteen children born to them, half that number passed into maturity and longer. Two died in infancy and one at six years of age. Of the remainder, either the date of birth is not recorded or the date of death, although it is known that one daughter, Mary married in 1831. It is of interest to note that there was a second 'Sarah's birth recorded, in 1791. The first Sarah had died in the year of her birth (1787). It seems to have been a practice in those days when lives could be cut short by illness or disease, to replace a deceased family member with one of the same baptismal name. Jane, although she died at only 39, at least married – Joseph Robinson, a Surgeon. Thomas died at the age of thirty three, in Valparaiso, another member of the family who travelled to far away places. The Jefferson 'Family Tree' and the Extracts from The Holy Trinity Church Records, both in the Appendix to this book, summarise what is known of the births and deaths date of the some of the family.

The oldest surviving child was Henry (2) who, like his Father, lived to the ripe old age of seventy seven. Robert (2), a future member of the business, born in 1785 – the year the Jefferson business commenced – died in 1848 at the age of sixty three years. So, the two children of Henry and Ann(e)'s union who became involved in the business lived the longest!

*At first Henry was described in the Church Records as a '**Mariner**' which was a fact. However, when his occupation changed to that of **Mariner and Merchant** (that is, after he opened the Wine and Spirits Merchants business in 1785) his occupation was changed to that of 'Merchant'. Henry was joined in the business, firstly by his eldest son Robert (2) – where they traded as Jefferson and Son, Merchants (Trade Directory for 1811); secondly by his second son Henry (2)(born 1800).*

Under Henry (1's) direction and total involvement, the business flourished, both the Whitehaven-based Wines and Spirits Merchants and also on the Shipping. There are interesting accounts of voyages made by Henry on their Vessel, the 'Thetis'. Brief extracts from the Ships' Log and Henry's Diary are reproduced in the Appendices section of this book. However, if the reader requires a more detailed account of Henry's involvement in ocean travel and life on Antigua, he is recommended to read that most excellent and informative book on Whitehaven's Sailing Fleets 'From Cumberland to Cape Horn' listed in the Selective Bibliography at the end of this book.

There is some ambiguity about Henry's homes. His address, where he and Ann(e) set up home, was 4 Cross Street, Whitehaven. He had *however, lived at another address previously – in Queen Street. When Ann(e), his wife, died in on 22nd May 1820, an address given was in Lowther Street. Yet, Henry died at home in 4 Cross Street in 1827!*

Henry was the first family member to subscribe to an organisation providing medical facilities for the townspeople of Whitehaven. The facility provided was named the Whitehaven Dispensary and Henry subscribed a half-guinea (10/6d = 5Op) per annum. Future generations of the Jefferson family would continue this practice in greater depth for more than one hundred years.

In 1802 Henry was elected to the Whitehaven Town and Harbour Board of Trustees (as would be some of his descendants). This Board was supported in Law by an Act of Parliament created during the reign of Queen Anne. Its purpose was to maintain and improve the infrastructure of the Harbour and the Town itself. The Lord of the Manor was always appointed; in the case of Whitehaven this was a member of the Lowther (Lonsdale) family who himself had the power to appoint six Trustees to the Board out of a total number of twenty one. The remainder – fourteen – had to be elected by ballot every three years. In a less than democratic system the Trustees were invariably appointed from amongst the wealthier citizens of the town, with a strong bias towards those connected directly or indirectly with the business of the Harbour. They could be Masters of their own Vessels, or Merchants dealing in goods which were liable to duties (Importers, etc.). A part-owner of a ship could also qualify to be a Trustee, provided that he owned not less than one-sixteenth of a Vessel registered at the Port of Whitehaven.

One small point is noted in a history of Cleator and Cleator Moor, in that Henry and an associate, Henry Fleming, were the sequestrators* of the old Wath Forge when the Smithy business owned and operated by John Colquhoun failed in 1786 and all his effects, fixtures, tools and implements were sold at the King's Arms, Whitehaven. So Henry had his finger in any number of pies.

On 1 June 1827, Henry retired from business. He was then seventy-seven years of age. All the Firm's customers were sent a circular notifying them of his retirement. It is interesting to read the content of this circular, as shown below:

My advanced age and declining health, having for some Years past prevented my taking an active part in Business, I have retired in favour of my Sons, whose conduct and attention, I doubt not, will render them worthy of a continuance of that confidence and support, which I have for so many Years experienced,

and for which I beg to return you my sincere thanks.

I am, with much respect,

Your obliged Servant

Henry Jefferson

ATTACHMENT TO THE ABOVE:

Whitehaven 1st June 1827

In consequence of the retirement of our MR HENRY JEFFERSON from business, we beg to announce to you, that the Concern will hereafter be continued under the Firm of ROBERT and HENRY JEFFERSON. We return you our best thanks for the confidence thereof to the new Firm.
Referring to you the annexed Circular of MR HENRY JEFFERSON

We remain

Your obliged Servants

Henry and Robert Jefferson

(Author's Note: This is typical of the 'flowery' language of those days; but that

notwithstanding, it is testimony to the confidence and trust Henry placed in his sons, that he unhesitatingly handed over the reins to his sons, for them to continue the business in the same successful manner as he had from its inception.)

Henry died in the year of his retirement (1827), a Widower, his wife Ann(e) having pre-deceased him by some seven years.

There are various conflicting reports on the number of children still alive at the time of Henry's death. He had fathered fourteen children as already stated, of whom two males, Robert (2) and Henry (2) had already entered the family business. The only other male child, Thomas, is recorded as living in South America. The future welfare of his remaining children, all female, was to be his main concern in his will.

The unmarried daughters, i.e. all excepting Jane (married to Joseph Robinson, a Surgeon) were deeded the following goods, chattels and services, presumably to share between them:-

All my Household Goods and Furniture, Plate, Linen, China, Wines and Spirits, Books and other Utensils and Things (sic) which may happen to be in or about my Dwelling House at the Time of my Decease and also my Carriage and such Horses as I may be possessed of at the

Time of my Death, with all my Hay, Corn and Provender for Horses, Saddles, bridles, Harness and Stable Utensils, together also with my Seat or Pew in Saint Nicholas Chapel in Whitehaven aforesaid and my Mortgage upon the Share of the Whitehaven Theatre with the Silver Ticket attached to it.

A codicil was appended with reference to Jane, the sole married daughter. He husband, Joseph Robinson, was one of the Executors of Henry's will and a separate Trust Fund was set up for her, barring Joseph from any gain from this Fund. The codicil was phrased as follows:-

'.........for her (Jane) sole and separate Use independent of her present or any future Husband and so that the same may not be subject to the Debts Control Contracts and Engagements of any such Husband'.

Thus did Henry protect his children from Fortune-Hunters.

Robert (2) was left Henry's gold watch, this having once belonged to Henry's Father-in-Law, Robert Tweedie, of Antigua.

A final twist in the will was a reference to a bequest for Robert (2), in respect of a legacy previously gifted to him by his Aunt Mary, Henry (1's) Sister (1764-1787). This legacy was in the amount of One Hundred and Fifty Pounds, which Mary had claimed had been allegedly bequeathed to her under Robert (1), Henry and Mary's Father's will. In as plain English as can be made of this convoluted matter, this would appear to be Henry's way of ensuring that there would be no dispute or controversy over this Legacy. On receipt of his Father's bequests to Robert(2), the latter was to a authorise a release from and claim on the £150, when called upon to do so by Henry's Executors. Failure to do so would disbar Robert from all benefits under Henry's will.

This codicil further emphasises Henry's sense of probity regarding his business and personal affairs.

Henry's Estate was valued at 'under £9,000.00' after his death.

He was interred at The Holy Trinity Church, Whitehaven.

*   **Sequestering**: possessing the authority to take legal possession of someone's assets until a debt has been paid.

CHAPTER
III

ROBERT JEFFERSON
(Robert (2))

Of: *Springfield, Bigrigg, Cumberland (previously resided at Keekle Grove, Whitehaven.*

Born: *Robert was born in 1785 (in Antigua) but was apparently baptised at Holy Trinity Church, Whitehaven He died at the age of sixty three on Sunday 24th September 1848.*

Son of: *Henry (1) Jefferson*

Education:

Nothing has been discovered regarding the education of these early generations of the Jefferson family. It is likely that they were either educated at home or attended local schools. Only later generations are recorded as receiving formal educations at famous institutions.

Non-business activities:

Robert became involved with the old Whitehaven

*Dispensary by first making an annual subscription of One Guinea whilst still in his early Twenties. In 1829 a Meeting was held in Whitehaven to promote the idea of building a local Infirmary. Robert, by then aged forty-four, together with his younger brother Henry (2), were co-opted as **Members** of a Committee. Robert was later chosen to be a **Vice-President** of this Committee, the obligation for this post being an annual subscription of Five Guineas. The site chosen was in Howgill Street and the Infirmary was duly built there on property purchased from Thos. Hartley (the Rope Maker). In February 1830 Five Fiduciary* Trustees were appointed, one of them being Robert. This had the effect of making the Trustees virtual proprietors of the Infirmary Buildings, a Trustee being appointed for life.*

(*Law involving Trust)

In the Town and Harbour Board elections of August 1820, Robert was elected to the Board but resigned in October of that year, sending a ambiguously worded letter to the Board, stating only that he **declined to continue as one of that body.** *The reason for his resignation has not been made public. However, Robert again stood for election to the Board in 1826 and again in 1829 but was not elected on either occasion; although the number of votes he polled on the latter occasion was the 15th highest, but only 14* *members were elected. However, in August 1832, he again succeeded in being elected and, from 1834, he acted as Chairman of the Board on numerous occasions.*

When, in 1837, the Town and Harbour Board required money for urgent improvements to the Harbour, Robert and Henry (2) provided the bulk of the funding for this purpose.

*Robert was appointed a **Justice of the Peace** in 1847 and was a Magistrate for the Allerdale Above Derwent Division.*

He was also involved with the old Whitehaven Junction Railway, from its earliest days, in conjunction with his Brother Henry (2) until his death, being appointed a Director and its first Chairman.

Military Connections:

A History of the family's overall involvement can be found in another Chapter of this book.

Family Business:

Robert followed his Father Henry (1), Founder of the business, into Trade, as a Merchant. In 1811 the name of the business according to local

directories of the time was known as Jefferson &
Son, Henry (1) and Robert (2) being the partners.
They traded as Merchants and Spirits Dealers,
Lowther Street, Whitehaven.

Henry (1) died in 1827.

By that time Robert had been joined in the
business by his younger brother Henry (2),
forming a partnership. In 1829, the trade
directories showed the business as trading as
Robert and Henry Jefferson, Merchants and
Importers, 27 Lowther Street, Whitehaven.

Family Life:

He married Elizabeth Brown with whom he had
***seven** children, four males and three females.*
*The second born child was **Henry (3);** the fifth*
***Robert (4).** Two of the children, William and a*
second child, also named William, died in
infancy. Elizabeth, born in 1832 married one
John Edward Weston

Robert's wife, Elizabeth, died in 1851.

The family lived at the handsome Gentleman's
residence of Keekle Grove, near Cleator Moor
for some time before 1839. Robert then
purchased Springfield House from Sir John
Ponsonby in 1841, after first taking a lease on

that property.   Please see Chapter XVI for details of the Jeffersons' properties.

Robert died in early Autumn 1848. A memorial stone was placed in the South transept of Egremont Church. His wife's name also appeared on this stone. However, the original Church was demolished in 1883 and a new Church was erected on the site of its predecessor within a few years.

All Headstones which had been placed against the Outer walls of the Church were removed and apparently broken up for use as 'hardcore', although this was local gossip at the time.

A recent visit to the Church confirmed that there are now no signs of any memorial plaques, slabs, headstones or anything relating to the Jefferson's connections with the Church.

In his will, which was extremely lengthy even for those times of rather ornate language, the family home (Springfield) was left to his son Henry (3), with the proviso that his (Robert's) widow Elizabeth had the right to continue living at Springfield for the rest of her life, provided she did not remarry. Elizabeth was also to receive an Annuity and allowances for the three daughters of the union, Mary (born 1821); Anne (born 1827); Elizabeth (born 1832). Mary was already married and Elizabeth was to marry shortly after her Father's death. Anne married some years afterwards. Robert provided legacies for the two younger sisters for their sole use independent of any husband they may later acquire. Mary received a marriage settlement, apparently in the sum of £1,000, plus a reduced legacy, all these on an annual basis.

On Robert's death his share of the business partnership passed to his son Henry (3). Robert (4) received his Father's shares in the Lumley Kennedy Shipbuilding business. Strangely though, Henry (3) had to pay for the value of Robert's holding in the business and Robert's Shareholding was made conditional to him being accepted by the other Shareholders in Lumley Kennedy.

Robert's Estate was valued for probate purposes, at 'under £20,000'. In 1848 that was an extremely large sum of money and proved his success as a businessman.

CHAPTER
IV

HENRY JEFFERSON, JP
(Henry (2))
(1800-1877)

Of: *(1) Lowther Street, Whitehaven;*
(2) Hensingham House, Whitehaven;
(3) then built Rothersyke, near Egremont

Born*:*   *17th July 1800 in Whitehaven,*
Cumberland.
Baptised at: *Holy Trinity Church, Whitehaven.*

Died: *19th July1877 and buried at St Bees*
Priory.
(see detailed report on the funeral at
the end of this Chapter).

Son of: ***Henry (1) Jefferson, the Founder***
of the Family Business

Educated at: *No record of this.*

Non-Business Activities:

For almost fifty years Henry Jefferson was
involved in the Town's affairs, both social and
political.

He served as an ex officio **Member** of the Whitehaven Board of Guardians, Union Rural Sanitary Authority and Highway Board.*

On 5th February 1829 a Meeting was held in the Black Lion Inn, Whitehaven, for the purpose of establishing a Joint Stock Bank (later renamed The Whitehaven Savings Bank). A Committee was appointed which included both the Jefferson brothers, Henry (2) and Robert (2). This association with the Bank continued for many years, Henry (3)(1823-1896) also being elected to the Board.

*In 1832 he was appointed to the Whitehaven Town and Harbour Board by the Earl of Lonsdale and was re-appointed in 1835. His brother, Robert (2) had already been a Member of the Board, but only briefly (**vide** Chapter III. Robert (2)).*

In that year (1832) Henry loaned the Trustees £2,000 in order that urgent improvements be carried out to the Harbour. Robert (2) donated a lesser amount. The combined contribution of the two brothers was about half of the required amount needed.

Henry supported the Second Earl of Lonsdale's candidate during the 1832 Elections of the Harbour Board of Trustees. Unfortunately, later, in 1846, Henry came into conflict with the Earl over Prime Minister Robert Peel's repeal of The Corn Laws. It was then that his loyalties switched from the Conservative Party to the Whigs (Liberals.) This aspect is more fully explained in Chapter Fourteen of this book.

*When the idea of the Whitehaven Junction Railway was first promoted, Henry Jefferson became actively involved and was one of its first **Directors** when that line was projected in 1844; along with other local notables, including his brother Robert (2) and members of the Lowther family.*

By 1845 a portion of the line from Carlisle had been completed but rail traffic could proceed only as far as Maryport. The Whitehaven to Maryport section was built in stages over the next two years (1845-1847), the two sections finally being completed in 1847, thus giving uninterrupted rail access to Carlisle from Whitehaven. A problem remained in that there was no connection between the Whitehaven Junction Railway, ending at Bransty Station, Whitehaven and the Whitehaven and Furness Junction Railway (from the South of the County) which ended at Preston Street, Whitehaven, a gap of about one mile. To solve this problem the Corkickle Tunnel was built, running under part of the Whitehaven Castle Grounds. This was opened in 1852. On this land, once part of the Castle Estate and now the local Park, can still be seen a castellated type of chimney, built for the purposes of allowing smoke to dissipate from the tunnel. The Whitehaven Junction Railway was acquired by the London and North Western Railway in 1866. This eventually became the London, Midland, Scottish Railway (the old L.M.S.)

In the General Election of 1857, the Liberal candidate for West Cumberland, Sir Wilfred Lawson, received support from Henry, who appeared with him on the Hustings# at Cockermouth. Again, in 1868, he again showed public support for the Liberal Party by walking through Whitehaven's streets to the Hustings arm in arm with the Liberal candidate. Mr Anthony Benn Steward.

*Henry was a serving **Magistrate (J.P.)** from 1851 for 26 years, until his death. He was originally nominated for the position of Justice of the Peace in 1835 but did not assume this post for another sixteen years.*

(*by virtue of one's position or status)

(#   A Meeting at which candidates in an election addresses potential voters)

Sporting Activities:

Henry was actively involved in the then extremely popular sport of Coursing and was the owner of a much celebrated greyhound named 'Judge'. In later life he ceased being an active participant in this sport yet maintained his visits to Coursing events, including the famed Waterloo Cup Meeting.

History has it that the greyhound was brought to Britain by the Romans.

There is a rhyme some hundreds of years old which extols the virtues of a classic greyhound's confirmation:

> "The head of a snake,
> The neck of a drake,
> A back like a beam,
> A side like a bream,
> The foot of a cat,
> And the tail of a rat."

Judge must have possessed at least some of the above characteristics to enable him to win the Waterloo Cup.

Military Connections:

None, although earlier and later generations of the Jefferson family were actively involved in the Westmorland and Cumberland Militia.

Family Business:

Henry (2) joined Jefferson & Son - Henry (1) who had founded the business in 1785, and his son Robert (2) – Robert being Henry (2's) elder brother.   At that time Henry (1) was Master of the Snow 'Gale', the first vessel of Jefferson's own fleet, purchased in 1775. The Jefferson's imported mainly tobacco, but also other goods then in demand, from Virginia into the Port of Whitehaven.   One can assume that any goods they exported were sold to Wholesalers in Virginia; tobacco etc. imported into Whitehaven was, likewise, sold to local Wholesalers.   They were also active in the importation of wines and spirits.

By 1829 the business had assumed its proprietary name of R(obert) and H(enry) Jefferson; Robert (1) had died in 1779. This name lasted for the duration of the family business which finally closed on 27th June 1998, after two hundred and thirteen years of uninterrupted trading as Wines and Spirits Merchants and Importers in the same family ownership throughout its history; claimed to be the oldest Family Wines and Spirits Merchants in the country.

Henry became directly and personally involved in the family's West Indies business Estates and this aspect is explained in detail in Chapters 8, 9 and ---.

Family Life:

Henry married Ann Davidson in 1824, at Holy Trinity Church. They had Nine Children, five boys and four girls, including Robert (3)(1826-1902) the eldest. Little is known of the birth and death dates of the remaining siblings, except that of Henry Thomas (born 1827; died 1874 – thus pre-deceasing his Father). He married one Mary Smith and they had at least one child, Henry. Charles (born 1829, died in 1852) also pre-deceased Henry (2) and Harriet (born 1837, died 1877) died in the same year as her Father. A 'Family Tree' in the Appendix Section of this book condenses the known information of the Jefferson family connections.

Ann died in 1854 but Henry did not remarry.

*Henry died suddenly on 19th July 1877, whilst attending a Meeting of the Whitehaven Board of Guardians, where he was an ex-officio Member of the Board. The Minutes of that particular Meeting recorded only that, in view of the sudden death of Mr Henry Jefferson JP of Rothersyke, further business be postponed until the next meeting, **except the Relief cases.***

The circumstances of Henry's death were the subject of much reporting in the local Press and, as such, deserve to be included in this brief biography of his life. The following are extracts from the Whitehaven News of 26th July 1877.

Awfully sudden death of Mr Henry Jefferson, of Rothersyke

The weekly meeting of the members of the Board (of Guardians) was held in the Old Public-office, Lowther Street, Whitehaven, on Thursday last (19th July 1877).

Present : Messrs Hodgson (Chairman), Fox (Vice-Chairman), Lindow, Smith, H. Jefferson (Rothersyke), Watson, Scambler, Spedding, Leech, Dickinson, Tyson, Reed, Rook, Carter, Musgrave, Porter, Dixon, Key, Bragg, C.Mossop, H. Mossop, H. Jefferson (Springfield), J.S. Ainsworth, Morton and Fletcher.

(Author's comments: Note all the familiar old West Cumbrian names. The main point of the Meeting was to discuss the proposed increase in the Salary of the Assistant Overseer for Arlecdon. Something more innocuous could have hardly been less worthy of the verbal contretemps which occurred, followed by the tragic death of a Member of the Board.

There were preliminary discussions before the onset of what were obviously bad-tempered exchanges between Henry (2) – whose nephew Henry (3)(Springfield) was also present at the

Meeting – and one Mr. Musgrave. **Reading between the lines there must have been some personal animosity between the two parties prior to this Meeting This was exacerbated by Musgrave alluding to Henry (2) only 'occasionally' attending Guardian Meetings. Reading the Minutes of the Meeting and the numerous 'Hear, hears' when Henry spoke, it is apparent that the Members' sympathies lay almost entirely with Henry.**

Mr. Musgrave had earlier been involved in an altercation with another Member, Mr. Scambler, who made an allegation of something being a 'bundle of lies from beginning to end.')

Extract:

Mr. H. JEFFERSON: I rise to order. Could these gentlemen not have attended that meeting if they had this large property? They are most respectable men, and they certainly might have attended the meeting. - The CHAIRMAN: You can ask the question when your time comes. – Mr.MUSGRAVE: It is not regular, but gentlemen who come here only occasionally do not know the rules of the place. – Mr. JEFFERSON: Not occasionally. – Mr. MUSGRAVE: Please to read the standing orders. Gentlemen who come here occasionally don't understand the rules. – Mr. JEFFERSON: Oh, indeed. Now, come get on. – Mr. MUSGRAVE; Are you done, sir? – Mr. JEFFERSON: Yes, I am. – Mr. MUSGRAVE: Oh, thank you.

Further discussion, then:

................Mr. H. JEFFERSON: Well, that might go to the Educational Committee. (Laughter.) – Mr. MUSGRAVE: Well, of course, only gentlemen who interrupt should take care that they are correct. – Mr.H. JEFFERSON: It will be a nice question for them at the next meeting. – Mr.MUSGRAVE: I'll wait till you're done, if it is until night. – Mr. H. JEFFERSON: Oh, I am done. – Mr. MUSGRAVE: Well, when will you begin again? – Mr. H. JEFFERSON: Not at all. – Mr. MUSGRAVE said that under that   pledge   he   would   go on...
....
Further discussion, then:

Mr. SPEDDING said that if that referred to him he would put Mr. Musgrave right. He was on the rate-book in three places. – Mr. MUSGRAVE said that Mr. Spedding was the gentleman referred to. – Mr. H. JEFFERSON: Name ! Name! You alluded to somebody in this room. - Mr. MUSGRAVE: I thought you said you were done? - Mr. H. JEFFERSON (to the Chairman): I appeal to your experience to say that that is actually incumbent upon him. – Mr.

MUSGRAVE: I asked you if you were done. I thought you said you were done before. - Mr. H. JEFFERSON: I ask you, Mr. Chairman, to ask Mr. Musgrave to name the individual in this room who addressed the meeting, and was not qualified. (Hear, hear.) - Mr. MUSGRAVE; You ought to know something at your time of life about public meetings. I said it was Mr Dalzell. – Mr. H. JEFFERSON: Mr. Dalzell is not here. (Voices, "Spedding, Spedding.") No, no; he said Dalzell. – Mr. MUSGRAVE, order being restored, further addressed the meeting for about a quarter of an hour or twenty minutes, recapitulating the objections against the advance, and repeating his suggestion for a deferred consideration. – Mr. WATSON said he was surprised to find that anyone would refuse an advance which would cost the ratepayers one-third of a farthing in the pound. – Mr. MUSGRAVE rose to speak, but his voice was drowned with the cries of "Order."- Mr. H. JEFFERSON: Are there not other gentlemen who wish to address the meeting? (Hear, hear) – Mr.MUSGRAVE: You're not Chairman yet. – Mr. H. JEFFERSON: I say it is quite out of order for you to reply to the observations of this gentleman here, at the present. (Hear, hear) – The CHAIRMAN: Well, but we don't think it so here. – Mr. MUSGRAVE read the by-law, which stated that every Guardian who spoke should stand and address the Chairman, and added: Now, he (Mr. Jefferson) sits there, chewing away. "And at all other times attend to the matter under consideration." (Mr. Jefferson had retained his seat whilst speaking, and had taken a lozenge or two at intervals.) – Mr. H.JEFFERSON: How many speeches is a man to make?   (Hear, hear.) – Mr.MUSGRAVE: Twice. Mr.Musgrave then proceeded to reply to Mr. Watson's observations at some length. He having resumed his seat, Mr. SPEDDING: I did not intend to say a word about this, but as Mr.Musgrave had taken it in hand, and he goes to Alfred Hodgetts and Fletcher - - Mr. MUSGRAVE? Do you know that? (Order, order.) It is a mistake; I did not go near. (Order, order.) – Mr. SPEDDING: We will have to go out, that will be the end of it, and leave the room to yourself. ("Hear, hear." and confusion.) – Mr.MUSGRAVE rose and endeavoured to make himself heard but failed, several Guardians maintaining cries of "Order", and "Chair." After a minute or two order was restored, and Mr. SPEDDING proceeded to say: I am not going to detain the Board as long as you (Mr. Musgrave) have done with a deal of unnecessary --.-- At this point Mr. H. Jefferson was observed to fall back in his chair, and the business of the meeting at once came to a standstill. Mr. Spedding stopped speaking, the windows were thrown open and fresh air admitted into the crowded and heated room. **(Author - in July?).** Those nearest to Mr. Jefferson at once loosened his neckcloth and collar, and made an attempt to lift him out of his chair and take him out of the room. This they failed to do, and they then lifted the chair containing Mr. Jefferson, who lay in a state of collapse, breathing slowly and stertorously, out of the room into the porch. Here some cold water was applied without avail, and medical aid having been called in from the moment of the attack, Dr. Dickson and Dr. Ablett came to the Board-room. Mr. Jefferson was removed to the room adjoining, tenanted by the keeper of the Old Public-office, and there, after an anxious pause, the doctors pronounced life to be extinct. In the meantime some of the members had returned to the Board-room, and there, on the motion of the CHAIRMAN, seconded by Capt. BRAGG, it was agreed to adjourn all the business excepting the relief cases to next Thursday.

Henry left a comprehensive will. He sold his half-share in the business to his son (Robert (3) for £1,750.00; and his house, Rothersyke, and effects for £500. Obviously this 'sale' was just a euphemism, possibly to avoid whatever taxes, inheritance, or whatever, being applied to his Estate.

Following his Father's example by making provision for the female side of the family, he made specific bequests to his daughters and grandchildren. The wording of his will in this clause was:

I also declare that all benefits given to any person under this my will who may be a female are intended for her own exclusive use and benefit, independent of or not to be subject to the debts control or Engagements of any husband Or husbands, (And that the receipts of any such female done notwithstanding Coverture+ shall be a sufficient discharge to my Trustees for any money paid to her by virtue hereof....

Put simply this clause safeguarded his daughters' bequeathed assets from any philanderer.

The total probate value of Henry's Estate was given as 'under £25,000).

(+ Protective or concealing covering the legal status of a married woman, considered to be under her husband's protection and authority.)

The Funeral:

The funeral took place on Monday 23rd July 1877, the cortege leaving from the deceased's home, Rothersyke, near Egremont, at 11.30am., heading for St. Bees, only a few miles away. Although the weather was very poor, with heavy rain, there was a large turnout, especially of most of the well known gentry of the district.

There was a total of eighteen carriages, four of which contained the chief mourners.

The immediate surviving family at the funeral consisted of Henry's eldest son Robert (3), and daughters Catherine (Kate) and Jane.

Strangely, the first carriage did not hold immediate family but, instead, held one officiating clergyman (Rev. Mr Gabbutt) and two Doctors (Dickson and Braithwaite). This carriage was followed by the hearse, behind which was the second carriage, holding the family mourners. The journey took over two hours to complete. It seems to have been the practice in those days for Gentlemen to send their carriage if unable to attend the funeral of one of their social standing; this signified their respect for the memory of the deceased and their sympathy with the family.

Included amongst the mourners was the High Sheriff of Cumberland, Mr Burns-Lindow, thus displaying the high esteem in which the decreased was held in the County.

The interment was conducted by Canon Knowles assisted by the Reverend Mr Gabutt..

It is interesting to note that the body of the deceased was enclosed in **three** coffins: an inner shell, a lead coffin and a polished oak outer *coffin, with brass mountings. The inscription on the oak coffin read:*

Henry Jefferson
of Rothersyke,
Born July 17th. 1800.
Died July 19th. 1877.

The deceased was then buried in the Churchyard of the Priory.

The Funeral arrangements were 'admirably' carried out by Mr. Jonathan Shepherd, Lowther Street, and Mr. Fisher of the Cab Company. (Whitehaven News)

*The cause of death was ascertained to be **quote** an affection of the heart **unquote**. No autopsy was carried out.*

From contemporary accounts it seems that Henry was a person endowed with great energy, He is described in newspaper accounts as having a 'burly, athletic frame...........with active habits.... despite his advanced years.   Note: (Seventy Seven years in the Nineteenth century was certainly looked upon as an 'advanced age.)

The Press were lavish in the platitudes bestowed on the deceased. He is described as having 'invincible determination, thorough manliness, courteous consideration, possessing straightforward honesty of thought and dealing'. Thus possessing 'national as well as individual qualities marking him as a representative Englishman!'

From study of the family history it is apparent that the qualities ascribed above to Henry (2) were identical to those possessed by both earlier and later generations of the Jefferson family.

CHAPTER
V

HENRY JEFFERSON
(Henry(3))

Of*:*   *Springfield, Bigrigg, Cumberland (now Cumbria)*

Born: 16 August   1823
Died: 27 November 1896

Son of*:*   ***Robert (2) Jefferson***

Educated at: *Harrow School*

Non-Business Activities:

Henry Jefferson was the oldest surviving **Magistrate** *of the Allerdale-above-Derwent Diuvision, qualifying as a Magistrate in January 1858. For many years he was* **Chairman** *of the Whitehaven Bench where he was esteemed as an 'able and judicious' Magistrate for almost forty years.*

He was created **Deputy-Lieutenant** *in 1879 and, in 1890, served the office of* **High Sheriff** *of the County.*

On the formation of the Cumberland County Council, Henry was co-opted onto the Police Committee and on the First Standing Joint Committee, the latter being composed of County Councillors and Magistrates.

*For a time he was **Chairman** of the Whitehaven Conservative Association and was also **President** of the West Cumberland Conservative Association. As a long-standing and consistent **Conservative** Henry Jefferson always appeared on the Conservative platform at election times. Although, generous in his financial support of the party he did not seek any prominent position at election times, partly, perhaps, because he was not a fluent orator.*

*Henry was **Senior Trustee** of the Whitehaven Savings Bank and one of the **Trustees** of the Whitehaven and West Cumberland Infirmary. He was also a **Governor** of St Bees Grammar School.*

*Other activities in which he was involved included being **Chairman** of the Board of the old Cleator and Egremont Railway. This line opened for goods traffic in January 1855 and for passengers in the summer of 1857. This line uthe line was transferred to the control of the Joint London and North-Western and Furness Companies in 1879.*

At the last Meeting of the Directors of the old Cleator and Egremont Railway, the Chairman, Henry (3) disclosed a surplus in the final account of £323.00, for disposal. One of the Directors suggested that this money be spent on a piece of 'plate' for the Chairman and Vice-Chairman; Henry, however, whilst thanking the Board for this kind gesture, suggested instead that this surplus cash be divided equally amongst the Members of the Board. The Chairman then intimated that the Directors would probably see their way to passing on their individual shares of this surplus to some deserving charity. There is no record as to whether or not the surplus was donated in this way.

A tradition of the old C & M Railway was to name each locomotive after the residence of a Director. Locomotive 13 0 – 6 – 0 ST was named 'Springfield', after Henry's house. This engine continued working until 1922.

*Henry was a **Director** of the Joint Stock Bank, the latter being a concern with which the Jefferson family had had a long association, ever since its inception.*

Sporting Activities:

Henry was very active in all the usual pursuits of a country gentleman. He was involved in the *local **Hunt** when it was operating, frequently running horses in their Cup Meetings at Harras Moor. He owned a Horse 'Tipperary Joe' in the 1850s which he ran with the Cumberland Foxhounds. Horse and Rider were apparently hard to beat over any going. His favourite colour for Horses was Grey of which, over time, he owned several.*

*Henry Jefferson was also a popular **Master** of the Whitehaven Harriers. He had assumed this position in 1861, taking over from his Father-in-Law Joseph Harris, who had been the Master for more than fifty years. Henry remained Master until 1879. The hounds were kennelled at his home, Springfield.*

*He was also a keen cricketer and was **Captain** of Whitehaven Cricket Club. His enthusiasm for the game was so great that he purchased a bowling machine for the club, in order to improve the team's batting standards. His colleagues, keen supporters and players of the game included gentleman of similar social standing; amongst them were Messrs. John Musgrave, Jos.Porter and .... Helder.*

Military Connections:

*Henry Jefferson was involved in the early days of the **'Volunteer'** movement, as had been his Father* *during the Napoleonic era. His service is chronicled in the 'Military' Chapter of this book, together with other family members.*

Family Business:

Following the death of his Father, Henry carried on business in partnership with his Uncle, Henry (2) (of Rothersyke), until the latter's death in 1877. Henry's cousin, Robert (3) (of Rothersyke) joined Henry in the business that year. Henry retired from the family business some years prior to his death and was replaced by his son Robert(5)(of Rosehill).

Family Life:

Henry married, firstly, in 1856 Mary the second daughter of Joseph Harris of Greysouthen. They had four children, two sons, Robert (5) (of Rosehill), Hugh (of St Helens) and two daughters, Mary and Elizabeth. Following the death of his wife, in 1864 Henry married Mary Gordon Watts, the daughter of James Gordon of Dumfries, by whom he two sons, Henry and Gordon. The second Mrs Jefferson and all the children were Henry's immediate surviving family.

Death and Funeral:

Henry died of 'apoplexy' at home, having been in failing health for some time. He had suffered a serious illness some years previously but had made a remarkable recovery, attributed to a 'fine constitution and regular and active habits of life'. Following a series of seizures he succumbed in the early morning of Friday 27 November 1896, in his seventy-fourth year.

'Apoplexy' was an expression used at the time to describe a cerebral haemorrhage or stroke.

His funeral took place on the Tuesday after his death, the cortege leaving Springfield at 1.30pm. There were numerous mourners, including most of the notables of the town of Whitehaven. Of interest is the fact that a carriage was provided for the servants of the house (the fourth in the procession). The first carriage was the 'Rosehill Brougham' containing Messrs. Helder and Brockbank (recognisable names even now, as important Solicitors in the town). There was again this peculiarity of non-relatives leading the cortege. In the second carriage were Henry's sons Robert (5) and Henry* (*not listed as a 'number' in the family tree). There is no mention of Henry's Widow (his second wife Mary (nee Gordon) in the list of mourners following the hearse.

The cortege duly arrived at Egremont Church where it was received by Three Clergymen who conducted the burial service. One of them was Henry's brother-in-law, the Reverend Miles Ponsonby Knubley, Rector of Staveley (he had married Ann(e) daughter of Robert (2), Henry's Father. Henry was interred in Egremont Churchyard; the Churchyard had closed in 1864 but was specially re-opened as there was a family vault there and Henry had reserved the right of interment in the vault, alongside his first wife, Mary who had died in 1861. A recent survey of the interior of the Church and the Churchyard has, however, revealed no trace of a Vault, nor of any physical reference whatsoever to the Jefferson family. The Rector of the Church has no knowledge of any Vault and can find no trace in the Church Records he has in his possession. It can only be presumed that renovations or alterations to the structure of the Church interior have concealed the Vault. By the time of Henry's death the present (new) Church had been erected on the site of the old one, so any destruction of the Vault during the building work at that time can be discounted.

The bearers were two of Henry's tenants plus his coachman and butler.

Complications subsequently emerged at the time of the disposal of his estate. Although Henry had made a will, with specific bequests, some bequests were also made in writing but not included in his will. Specific problems now arose over several of these informal bequests, especially as regards the inheritance of certain items of silver. The outcome was a split between two factions of Henry's family:

(1) Henry's surviving second wife Mary Watts Jefferson (nee Gordon) and her children Henry Watts and Gordon;

(2) Henry's 'first' family, sons Robert (5), (Joseph) Hugh, Mary and Elizabeth, by his late wife Mary (nee Harris).

Solicitors became involved in the family quarrel over the will which indicates that had become quite bitter. The outcome was not revealed.

(Gordon took no part in the running of the business - he was can electrical engineer living in Liverpool - and his Mother later returned to her pre-marital home in Dumfries).

One of the informal bequests made in writing Is shown hereunder:-

I wish Robert (5) to have the old gold watch 'Tweedie'* and seals attached……...
I wish Henry (Watts) to have the gold watch I wear given to me by my father-in-law Mr Gordon and Gordon the gold chain attached with locket

etc. except the gold Napoleon which I should like Hugh to have it belonged to his late Mother and Robert her wedding ring which I have always worn on my right little finger.............

Thus, personal gifts were deeded to Henry's four sons from both marriages.

Henry's partnership had already passed to his son Robert (5) on Henry's retirement from business some years prior to his death. When Robert (3) retired, Hugh joined Robert (5) in the business and it was again run by brothers.

> ** This watch must have been given to Henry (1)(1750-1827) by his Father-in-Law, Robert Tweedie of Antigua.*

CHAPTER
VI

ROBERT JEFFERSON, J.P., D.L.
(Robert (3))

Of: *Rothersyke, near Egremont*

Born: 1826
Died: 1902

Son of: *Henry (2) Jefferson*

Educated at: *No trace found*

Non-Business Activities:

*In the family tradition Robert also served as a **Magistrate** from October 1877 - for the Allerdale Above Derwent Division.*

*Robert was also appointed a **Deputy Lieutenant** (D.L.) of the County.*

In the 1890s he sat on the Whitehaven Board of Guardians Assessment Committee, following a precedent set by his forebears.

*When the first Cumberland County Council came into being in 1889, Robert was elected as a **Councillor**; this was followed by his being elected a **County Alderman**. He retired from the* *latter post in 1895, the post being a six-year appointment only. Records show that Robert's attendance at Meetings was spasmodic, those held in Whitehaven being the ones he was most likely to attend.*

The 'Whitehaven News' weekly newspaper (still highly active after more than one hundred years) was introduced in 1881 and 120 shares were offered for sale in this venture, at £50.00 per share. Robert purchased a number of these shares but, when his estate was wound up after his death in 1902, no such shares were listed in the estate. It is likely therefore that he had disposed of them during his lifetime, as he was active in the Stocks and Shares Market.

Other ventures in which he became a Shareholder involved Railways, another sphere in which the Jefferson family had been involved since the earliest days. Robert was an investor in the Cleator and Workington Junction Railway and the Maryport and Carlisle Railway. Not only local, but National Railway systems were also subject to his investment as his estate papers later revealed. As regards his investment in the Cleator and Workington Junction Railway, the name of his house 'Rothersyke' was given to one of the locomotives.

Sporting Activities:

No record of his active involvement in organised sports or the usual family pursuits of Coursing, Steeplechasing, Hound Trailing, etc.

Military Connections:

None.

Family Business:

Robert became a partner in the family business, with his cousin Henry (3) in 1877, replacing his Father, Henry (2) who had died that year,

Family Life:

Robert never married.   He inherited Rothersyke from his Father, Henry (2).   As there were no heirs to the property it was sold after Robert's death in 1902.

It seems that Robert led a rather bland life, not participating in any active social pursuits.   His energies seemed to be directed towards involvement in civic and business affairs.

Robert's estate was valued at £22,000, relatives benefiting from legacies.   He also left £100 to the

Whitehaven and West Cumberland Infirmary for
who he had served as Fiduciary* Trustee.

*Fiduciary: **Law involving trust, especially**
              with regard to the relationship
              between a trustee and a
              beneficiary.

CHAPTER
VII

JOSEPH HUGH JEFFERSON

Of: *St. Helens, Cockermouth*

Born: 1859
Died: 1920

Son of: *Henry (3) Jefferson*

Educated at: *St. Bees Grammar School (?)*

Non-Business Activities:

In his youth Hugh spent some years Ranching in Wyoming, U.S.A.

Hugh followed the usual practice of his forebears by being appointed a **Justice of the Peace.**

He was also a member of the Cockermouth District Council.

Sporting Activities:

A steeplechaser of note; in the late Eighteen Eighties, Hugh won the Cumberland Foxhounds Point-to-Point race.

*He was **Secretary** to the Cumberland Hunt and to the West Cumberland Otter Hounds, and 'whipper-in' with his brother (Robert(5)) with the Whitehaven Harriers.*

Military Connections:

Hugh joined the Westmorland and Cumberland Yeomanry in 1891. Full details of Hugh's association with the Yeomanry can be found in a separate Chapter of this book.

Family Business:

When Robert (3) Jefferson, of Rothersyke, retired in 1896, Hugh, brother of Robert (5) joined the family business. Thus the business once again reverted to being controlled by two Brothers.

*Apart from family business connections, Hugh Jefferson was also a **Director** of Messrs. Jennings Bros.Limited, Cockermouth.*

Family Life:

In 1888 Hugh married Miss Elizabeth Ann Dixon, daughter of Mr. Dixon of Rheda, Frizington. They had two daughters: Mary (born 1889); she married a Captain McDonald in 1914. The second daughter – Rheda Kathleen, was born in 1890 and married a Captain Robert A. Gordon in 1911. Captain Gordon was killed in action in 1914, the very early days of the First World War, (The 'Great War').

Little else has been recorded about Hugh Jefferson.

CHAPTER
VIII

ROBERT JEFFERSON, JP, CA
(Robert (5))

Of: *Firstly, Rosehill, Whitehaven, then inherited Springfield, Bigrigg, Cumberland) following the death of his Father.*

Born: *?   ?   1857*
Died: *31ˢᵗ May 1942*

Son of*:* ***Henry (3) Jefferson,** JP, DL*

Educated at*: Harrow School*

Non-Business Activities:

*Robert was appointed a **Magistrate (J.P.)** in 1891 and, for 19 years, was Deputy Chairman of the Whitehaven Bench. In 1930 he succeeded Mr W McGowan as **Chairman**, an office he held until January 1942.   On his retirement he was presented with a silver salver by his fellow Magistrates.   Robert Jefferson was noted for his fairness when presiding on the Bench but could be severe on those who were found guilty of cruelty to children or animals; or on others who had committed mean-spirited crimes.*

*In 1904 he was elected **County Councillor** for Egremont (North) Division, a post he held until his death. (his son Henry later represented Egremont (North) as County Councillor). He was elected **Alderman** in 1917, serving in this capacity for several years. As a County Councillor he was a member of the **Joint Standing Committee;** and also served as a **Special Constable**. In his first ten years as a County Councillor, Robert's attendance record was almost 100%.*

*Robert Jefferson displayed a great interest in Education and the advancement of young people and he was involved in several areas. In 1904 he was elected **Chairman** of the Egremont Group of Schools, was a **Governor** of St Bees Public School and also, for many years, a **Governor** of Whitehaven County Secondary School. His involvement was not just in name only; conscious of his responsibilities by taking on these duties, he carried out personal visits during school hours.*

*Notwithstanding the commitments described above, Robert Jefferson also became involved in Hospital work. He held the office of **President** of the West Cumberland District Nursing Association and was a **Trustee** (one of the oldest) of the Whitehaven and West Cumberland Hospital.*

*From 1886 he was a **Trustee** of the Whitehaven Savings Bank.*

Sporting Activities:

*Hound Trailing was a special love for Robert Jefferson and no-one did more for the Sport during his lifetime. He was the **Founder** of the **Hound Trailing Association** in 1909 and was unanimously re-elected **President** at every annual meeting from its founding. As a fairly successful owner, one of his hounds, Climber, won the HTA trophy in 1912, and another, Leader, won in 1940. Yet another of his hounds, Dalesman, was the winner of Lord Leconfield's Cup in 1906. Robert Jefferson was also involved with Tommy Dobson, Founder and Master of the Eskdale Foxhounds ; he was **Master** of the **Whitehaven Harriers** until it was disbanded in 1901.*

*Although Hound Trailing remained the main sporting interest for the last 40 years of Robert Jefferson's life, it was not his only leisure pursuit. He was, at one time, one of the **leading steeplechase riders** in the country and won many races throughout the North of England. His famous Mare, St. Bridget, won many races at Harras Moor, Cartmel, Dumfries and Carlisle. and was considered unbeatable by any other horse with the exception of one, 'Old Joe' a horse which won the Grand National in 1886. On most occasions however, St. Bridget beat Old*

Joe. St. Bridget's racing career finished in 1887 but Robert bred a gelding, Balcary, from her. Balcary went on to win more than 20 races throughout the Northern Counties. Unfortunately, Robert's racing career ended at Carlisle when his horse, Beggar Boy, stumbled and rolled on him, the injuries forcing him to retire from steeplechasing.

Robert Jefferson was a keen cricketer and, as a young man, he played for the Gentlemen of Cumberland team; for more than 30 years he was **President** *of Egremont Cricket Club. As* **President** *of the Egremont Recreation Club he presided at the opening ceremony of the club's pavilion in 1909.*

Some of Robert's personal correspondence has survived, covering the period 1889-1905. Much of it is concerned with Horses, especially the buying and selling of horse, entering races, the organisation of hunts and Robert's role as a Director of the Whitehaven Race Stand Company; and sport in general.

Military Connection:

Robert Jefferson joined the **Westmorland and Cumberland Yeomanry** *in 1885, at the age of 27. Full details of Robert's involvement with the Yeomanry can be found in a separate Chapter of* *this book, dealing with the family's Military connections.*

Family Business:

For 64 years Robert Jefferson was involved in the family business of Wine and Spirit Merchants. This business had been started in 1785 and remained in the family in an unbroken line through five generations. After five years in the Company's employment, as Jefferson's representative in London and Spain, Robert joined the family partnership, with his brother Hugh and was Head of the firm from 1896. When Hugh died in 1920, Robert's son, Henry (4) became a partner in the firm.

The firm's business activities were spread all over the world. In addition to owning plantations in the West Indies, for many years the firm owned its own shipping fleet.

Amongst papers found after Robert's death, was correspondence (1889-1905), dealing with his involvement in a Tobacco agency, in association with a Mr. Alfred M. Simon. This business was run separately from the family business of R & H Jefferson.

The history of Jefferson's business activities, at home and abroad, will be dealt with in depth in separate Chapters of this book.

In 1924, Robert took his son Henry into the partnership and, in recent years, the latter has carried on most of the active work in the firm.

Family Life:

In 1894 Robert married Miss Constance Lumb (Lamb?) of Wray Castle, Westmorland and Homewood, Whitehaven. (The latter residence was, unfortunately, demolished some years ago but the writer remembers it well, as an imposing residence constructed of St Bees Sandstone).

Robert and Constance lived for many years at Rosehill, Moresby. Tragically, Mrs Jefferson died in 1926 and this was an extremely severe blow to Robert. His most happy married life was perhaps the reason for his benevolent and caring attitude towards women and children, some in reduced circumstance, who appeared before him in Court.

Many tributes were paid to Robert on his passing, from friends, colleagues, the Bench, Police and the local Press. It is perhaps a measure of the man that, shortly before his death, he attempted to retire from Public Life, as Chairman of the Probation Committee, but had been prevailed upon to continue in the position.

As an indication of Robert's character, letters found amongst his private papers, reveal that he could be extremely stubborn when his rights had apparently been violated. He carried on a correspondence with Barrow Agricultural Society for over three years over a prize he had won (in 1888) and did not receive until 1891.

His idiosyncratic way of closing letters was most amusing:

***'Believe me'** followed by **'Yours e.t.c.'**, and not always at the closing of his letters.*

His handwriting (signature?) is that which appears on Jefferson labels for their famous own-blend Rum, brandy and whisky (see Appendices).

Robert was at buried at Egremont Cemetery on Thursday June 4th 1942, following a Service at St.John's Church, Bigrigg.

CHAPTER
IX

The Family Business

Numerous artefacts from the old business are still to be seen at 'The Rum Story' Exhibition, in Jefferson's original premises on Lowther Street, Whitehaven.

They include the following interesting items:

A Corking Machine of French origin. Corks printed with the name 'Jefferson's' were kept in a specially designed cabinet in the Shop.

There is also a Giant 'Jefferson Barrel' which could hold 1,720 Gallons (7,819 litres) of Rum. At today's price a full barrel would cost in excess of £250,000.00

JEFFERSON'S BONDED WAREHOUSE

All imported goods were held in Bond until re-exported or, as in the case of the Jefferson's Warehouse, duty paid.

One of the reasons for the success of a Bonded warehouse in Whitehaven and for the success of the Jefferson's business was its geographical location. The West coast of England was the perfect landing point for goods from the Caribbean so, naturally, a Bonded Warehouse would grow at the place of importation. During its busiest days the Warehouse would be full of goods of all kinds. Especially purpose built casks for transporting alcoholic liquids, especially Rum.

The Warehouse was dimly lit and for the employees there was hard and unremitting work. They would not be conscious of the time of day as there were no windows. All barrels had to be manhandled, regardless of size. They would need to be hoisted, weighed and checked before being sorted for distribution.

There was a non-stop cycle of receipts and deliveries.

A small office, set in a corner of the Warehouse, served as space for a clerk who attended to the ledgers and also supervised the ongoing work.

COOPERS' YARD

Jefferson's made its own Barrels, of all regulation sizes. A description of the various capacities can be found in the Appendix to this book ('Vessels').

A sign in the Coopers'; Yard read:

'NOISE AND SPEAKING WILL NOT BE TOLERATED'.

In today's workplaces it would be impossible to find such signs, or even envisage any being there in the first place.

CHAPTER
X

The Company's Shipping Business

Henry (1) Jefferson (1750-1827), was the eldest surviving son of the Patriarch of the Family, Robert (1)(1704-1779). Both he and his Father were primarily Master Mariners involved in Shipping and as Merchants, where they imported into Whitehaven, Tobacco from Virginia and Molasses, Sugar and Rum from the West Indies. They chartered vessels for this purpose and sailed these as Masters in their own right. Early on in their joint venture they purchased the first of their fleet of vessels, the Snow (Brig) 'Gale'.

Details of the 'Gale' its voyages and related information, as well as the others in the Jefferson's Fleet are listed and described in the Appendices section of this book. In the Eighteenth and early Nineteenth centuries Whitehaven was one of the most important ports in England; estimated to be the sixth most important after London.

Henry (1) extended the scope of their activities by expanding the business into Wholesale and Retail Wine and Spirits Merchants, late in the 18th

Century (in 1785), thereby becoming the actual Founder of the Firm of Jefferson's. In those days Whitehaven had a direct foreign and colonial trade in general merchandise and was known as the 'Cumberland Liverpool' of its day because of its relative prosperity to the rest of the country. The grand Merchants' houses in the town gave substance to this statement. Some of these are still in existence though, unfortunately, either no longer used as residences or else, in some cases, their classic features distorted by poor maintenance, slipshod conversion or gaudy paintwork.

In due course Robert (2)(1785-1848) and Henry (2)(1800-1877), both sons of Henry (1), assumed control of the business as partners in R & H Jefferson.

As the Jefferson's were Merchants there was a basic necessity to import and thus permanent shipping availability was of paramount importance to their business. Most of the Company's Ships were built in Whitehaven. In all the family owned ten ships, but never more than three at one time. They maintained this shipping fleet until the 1870s when the trade was all but lost to Liverpool. The explanation for this serious loss was that there were insufficient means for rapid disposal of cargoes at Whitehaven to cope with current demand. There is also some substance in the story that the shallow draught of the Port meant that ships of larger tonnage could not enter the harbour.

To meet demand they also chartered other ships from time to time. Of the ten owned by the family, all were involved, at one time or another, in trade with the West Indies, predominantly Antigua but also Jamaica. They imported the basic produce of those countries, mainly Sugar, Molasses and Rum. The demand for these items in England was extremely high and the competition was fierce. For a Merchant to have his own Vessels gave the Jefferson's a head start in their business enterprises, hence the importance to them of having full control over their Vessels. They had this in their own fleet of course; when necessary, due to volume of trade, they chartered other Vessels. The family were also sailing to Brazil, Buenos Aires,

Some of the Masters of their Fleet were local born and highly experienced in the Shipping World. Captain Joseph Wise who, at one time, was Master of the 'Lady Shaw Stewart' and also sailed the 'British Queen' as regular Master was heavily involved with the Jefferson family. The Wise family, originating in Cockermouth, has a long and notable involvement with seafaring, connected with Cumberland, especially with Whitehaven.

Also, Captain Thomas Kennedy, who was Master of the 'British Queen' between 1838 and 1845 sailed Jefferson vessels for many years.

Both the above vessels were either owned, in whole or part, by the Jefferson's, or registered in their names. Between them Captains Wise and Kennedy did numerous crossings to Antigua from Whitehaven, on behalf of the Jefferson's. They carried Rum, Sugar and Molasses, the usual cargoes loaded in Antigua.

On occasions, the Jefferson's 'switched' Masters from one vessel to another. This would depend upon the availability of the Masters for particular voyages as sometimes they had other business to attend to, usually connected with the world of Shipping and Trade.

Captain Joseph Wise is commended in the 'Cumberland Pacquet' of January 1847 for sailing the 'British Queen' in a record passage between Whitehaven and Antigua, via Belfast, in forty-three days. He is also noted for carrying out three voyages between Whitehaven and Antigua in one year – a remarkable feat!

Apart from the normal hazards of sailing the Atlantic Ocean in all weathers, there was the additional problem of disease which was rampant and almost endemic in some of the Ports they visited, including those in the West Indies.

Malaria, Yellow Fever and Cholera were
commonplace and caused the deaths of a number
of sailors connected with the Jefferson Fleet.

Pirate vessels were also a threat and Captain
Thomas Kennedy encountered a suspiciously
acting vessel during a voyage as master of the
'British Queen' in August 1842. Astute
seamanship and navigation enabled him to avoid
contact. His reports on this incident and also
other adventures he experienced during his
period sailing the Jefferson vessels – including a
disastrous earthquake at Antigua in 1842 – were
meticulously recorded and details can be found
in the book 'From Cumberland to Cape Horn',
listed in the Bibliography at the end of this book.

CHAPTER
XI

The Yeaman's Estate, Antigua and other properties owned by the Jefferson family on Antigua

Herewith a brief description of ANTIGUA where the Jefferson family maintained their Estate(s).

Antigua is a sub-tropical island and part of the Leeward Islands in the Eastern Caribbean. Although it has a drier climate than most other islands in the West Indies it is still subject to tropical storms and hurricanes between June and November. The capital is St John's.

It was first settled by the English of neighbouring St. Kitt's in 1632, and, within a century, the English settlers had totally supplanted the indigenous Caribbean inhabitants.

Most of the inhabitants of Antigua are descendants of African slaves brought to the island in the late Seventeenth century to work for the British on sugar plantations.

Sugar was then a much sought after crop for cultivation and export to Britain as it was not grown throughout the world to the extent it is today, there being just a handful of producers including the Portuguese on the island of Madeira.

The Slave Trade was abolished in 1807 and the abolition of Slavery itself throughout the British Empire followed in 1833/4.

A major advantage for Antigua is the fact that it boasts deep bays and secluded inlets. This made it ideal for both the loading and unloading of ships which was probably one of the reasons why the Jefferson's settled on Antigua for their expansion.

Antigua became self-governing in 1967 and fully independent in 1981.

Sugar cane remains the Island's main export and has been the staple of the economy since the Seventeenth century.

Tourists have now discovered the Island, especially the white sandy beaches of the South-Eastern peninsula. However, the Island is still relatively unspoiled and uncrowded, with a relaxed, authentic atmosphere.

ESTATES

The Jefferson family acquired their Estates, principally Yeaman's on the 28th August 1832 *from the estate of Sir John Ogilvy of Inverquharity, Forfar, Scotland. The signatures of the Purchasers. Robert*(2)(1785 – 1848) and Henry (2)(1800-1877) Jefferson are affixed to the Conveyancing Indenture.*

* Robert was born on the Island of Antigua.

Yeaman's *is located on the West shore of the present Potworks Lake (a Dam), near the centre of the Island of Antigua.*

BRIEF HISTORY OF YEAMAN'S

Extracts from the History of the Island of Antigua

JEAFFRESON

18$^{th.}$ March 1624:   The Ship 'Hopewell' fitted out by Ralph Merifield, commanded by Captain John Jeaffreson (a Suffolk man).

13$^{th.}$ September 1625: In the event of Thomas Warner's decease, John Jeaffreson (if still living) to be appointed Lieutenant.

Consult the papers of Christopher Jeaffreson, Agent for St.Kitts, embodied in 'A Young Squire of the 17$^{th.}$ Century, by John Cordy Jeaffreson, 1878 (re treatment of **'white'** *slaves.)*

*2nd. May 1782: Jno (sic) Shirley suspended Mr.
Jeaffreson of the Council for saying "The King
should do what he pleased with his Privy Council
and that he had to corrupt Parliament go give
him a sanction for it, or words to that effect,"
and "Why, you yourself think so too, don't you?"*

(He was reinstated and the Governor was asked
not to act too harshly.)

Author's Note: The above passages have
been included solely because of the similarity of
the two names: **'Jeaffreson'** and **'Jefferson'**.
The coincidence is strange, although no
connection between the two families has been
established: there are similar names, apparently
similar seagoing occupations and also connection
with Antigua.

YEAMANS

*The following are extracts from the History of the
Island of Antigua by Vere Langford Oliver,
MRCS, Eng., LRCP, London.   They are not
relevant to the Jefferson family but are included
to show the convoluted History of the Yeamans
and their association with the Island and other
families.*

Elizabeth, daughter of William Yeamans was married at St. Paul's (Antigua?) in 1737 to Samuel Eliot.

Descendants of Elizabeth and Samuel Eliot (grandchildren) were Elizabeth Yeamans Eliot (died at Blinfield, Berkshire, 30 September 1829) and Rachel Yeamans Eliot – married in 1805 to Daniel William Mackinen of Antigua and Blinfield, Berkshire. He died in January 1829.

Elizabeth Rachel Ann Yeamans, daughter of William Yeamans, under 17 on $22^{nd.}$ February 1761, married William Yeamans Archbould. (His will dated $22^{nd.}$ February 1761 – then of Bristol – proved PCC $7^{th.}$ April 1763.) Married secondly Sir James Laroche, Bart. December 1764. She died $27^{th.}$ January 1781, buried in Stapleton Church.

Mrs Frances Yeamans married Nicholas Collins on $9^{th.}$ April 1741 in the Parish of St.Paul's.

Henrietta, daughter of Governor John Yeamans married Richard Ash, before 1717. She was the god-daughter of Governor Christopher Codrington, Captain-General of H.M.'s Leeward Charibbee (sic) Island.

Mary, daughter of John Yeamans of Mill Hill, Old Road, Antigua, Lt. Governor of that Island.

Widow of Nathaniel Sampson; married at St. John's, Antigua, on 30th. October 1701. Five Children – the third Yeamans Byam Sampson died at about age of 12, buried at St. Aldate's Oxford, 24th. June 1714.

Jno Yeamans signed the proclamation of George I on Queen Anne's dearth on 1st. August 1714.

(Additional Source: Goodwin family, previous owners, still resident on Antigua: February 2005)

Ownership: The following information was supplied by Rosemary Magoris (nee Goodwin), the daughter of the last recorded owner, George Alfred (Alfie) Goodwin, in February 2005. According to her records, the date the Jefferson's acquired ownership of Yeaman's was 1878. This is considerably at variance with the date shown on the Conveyancing Indenture – 28th August 1832. The signatures of both Robert (2) and Henry (2) Jefferson were affixed to this Indenture. As Robert (2) died in 1848 and Henry (2) in 1877, it is not possible that they could have been the Purchasers of the Estate in 1878. By that date, the Jefferson Family Business was being run by Henry (3) (1823-1896) and Robert (3) (1826-1902). This aspect is currently being investigated by the descendants of the Goodwin family.

First recorded:	*Captain John Yeamons* (sic)
1750:	*Shoot Yeamans*
1790	*Hyslop & Greenough*
1829	*Messrs. Ruckers*
1843	*J. Wood & Bennett*
1878	*R.H. Jefferson***
1891	*William Goodwin*
1921	*George Alfred (Alfie) Goodwin.*

It is recorded in the Goodwin family archives that, in 1852, Yeaman's consisted of 210 acres and had 110 slaves. This again, is a matter for argument. The Slave Trade had been abolished by then (see paragraphs on Antigua), almost twenty years previously.

*The other Estates owned by the family were: **Yorks** and **New Division**. These Estates were also purchased, in 1832, from the Ogilvy family. The Jefferson's also had financial interests in **Jolly Hill Estate, Golden Grove and Greencastle.***

Through their shipping interests they transported sugar to England for such families as the Codringtons, the Jarvis's, the Nugents, and others. When sugar prices became depressed (through over-supply) they began buying up

*molasses on the Island for their own purposes –
the production of Rum – reputed to be the best
Rum available in England!*

*Four Hundred Slaves were listed on the
indenture and were treated thereon as items of
stock. However, Slaves on the Jefferson's
Antiguan Estates were among the first to be
freed, but this fact and the passage of more than
two centuries does nothing to lessen the dramatic
impact of this indenture of workers. There is no
record that the Jefferson family sent any Slaves
to the United Kingdom. However, the date of
purchase of the Estate (28/8/1832) was very close
to the date of the total abolition of slavery
through the British Empire (1833/4) so one
cannot see much kudos for the family in their
freeing of the slaves, just the anticipation of an
event which was to have much positive effect
upon working conditions, quality of life and
humanitarianism through the West Indies..*

*In the Eighteenth century (and of course for
many years prior, during the hated slave-trading
days), life for the employees (Slaves) was less
than pleasant. Although the Plantation Owners
provided accommodation this was rudimentary,
of an extremely low standard and quite unfit for
inhabitation by European standards. The Slaves
generally elected to build their own houses on the
Plantation where they worked. These followed
the traditional styles of dwellings found in*

whatever homeland they had been forcibly abducted from. They were generally 'long houses', of wattle and daub (mud and plaster), with earth floors and thatched with palm leaves.

Work on the Plantations was always arduous, entailing long hours, unremitting toil and in working conditions quite insufferable most times - oppressive heat and high humidity. The Plantation Owners employed ethnic 'Slave Drivers' (hence the term in common usage today but now totally misapplied); they were equipped with whips which they did not hesitate to use. This form of control was more or less guaranteed to maintain and even increase productivity. Collapse from heat exhaustion in the workshops was common, a form of 'dropsy'. Other tropical illnesses were also rife, including malaria as the island was in those times heavily infested with malarial-carrying mosquitoes.

However, for the benefit of the Owners, the island proved ideal for the growing of sugar cane. It had rich, heavy soils, tropical heat and high humidity, all prerequisites for producing abundant crops of sugar.

Sugar plantations had been established by Sir Christopher Codrington in 1674, to meet the growing demand in Europe for this product. The island was cleared for cultivation – back-breaking work in that climate, removing thick shrubs and undergrowth with which the island was covered. It eventually boasted of having 160 Plantations.

Despite periodical tropical rainstorms there was a constant shortage of freshwater and, in 1731 a Bucket of Water would sell for 3/- (three shillings = 15p).

The Jefferson's had an Agent, Mr. Bispham, based on Antigua in the 1850s, whilst they were exporting Rum and Sugar to Whitehaven. By 1859, the Jefferson-owned Brigantine 'British Queen' was plying between Whitehaven and Antigua and did so for over twenty years, for the same purpose. George C. Bispham, a member of a well-known Barbados family looked after the Jefferson's interests on Antigua, primarily the Yeaman's Estate.

According to information received from reliable sources on Antigua (Archive material) Thomas Jefferson's Grandfather is buried at the old Anglican Church, in Old Roadtown, near his plantation. Therein lies a puzzle: The only 'Thomas's' located in the Family Tree are :

Thomas: Born 1749; died 2nd January 1770. Buried in Holy Trinity Churchyard. Son of Robert (1)(1704-1779) who is recorded as buried in Holy Trinity Churchyard

Thomas is Grandson of: ?
Thomas is also recorded as buried
in Holy Trinity Churchyard

Thomas: *Born 2nd August 1802/3?*
                Died 1836, in Valparaiso
                Son of Henry (1)(1750-1827)
                Henry (1) buried at Holy Trinity
                Churchyard
                Thomas is Grandson of Robert (1)
                (buried at Holy Trinity
                Churchyard)

Henry Thomas: *Born: 1827*
                Died: 1874
                Son of Henry (2)(1800-1877)
                Henry (2) buried at St. Bees
                Priory
                Henry Thomas is Grandson of
                Henry (1) (buried at Holy Trinity
                Churchyard.

None of the above therefore qualify as being the Grandson of the 'Grandfather of Thomas' buried on the Island. So who is the mystery 'Grandfather' and who is the equally mystery 'Thomas'? It must be a relative of the 'John Jeaffreson (a.k.a. 'John Jefferson') mentioned elsewhere, both in this narrative and in Antiguan Archives. No relationship has been established between this Antiguan Jeaffreson/Jefferson (the Patriach, John, was born in Suffolk, England)

and the Cumbrian Jefferson family. Nevertheless, it is strange that similar names on a small Island were not related.

Recent further information received from a descendant of a family (the Goodwins) who were once owners of Yeamans Estate (post Jefferson's ownership) has revealed the following information relative to Robert and Henry Jefferson:

They owned 32 acres in St. Paul's Parish, Antigua between 1852 and 1871. Yeamans Estate is in St. Peter's Parish and, in 1871, the Jefferson's are recorded as owning 120 acres in this Parish, apart from the 209 acres comprising Yeamans Estate itself. There is some dispute in this respect; it may be that the person recording these two different plots of land was confused as to the size of Yeamns. Other documentation reports the size of Yeamans as 209/210 acres and there is no report of any sub-division of land on the Estate.

In the accounts of Slave Compensation claims for the Colony of Antigua, in October 1835, Robert and Henry Jefferson are recorded as having received £2,342.2s.0d. in return for their emancipation of 146 slaves. A further amount of £4,549.5s.10d. was paid on 5th. October 1835, as compensation for the similar emancipation of 309 slaves.

In the 'Illustrations' section of this book there are several photographs relating to the Yeaman Mansion. Firstly as it appeared in the 1930s; then a photograph of a large Windmill in the grounds of the Mansion and within sight of the House and, thirdly, sadly, the Yeaman's Plantation it is now - in ruins.

Also in 'Illustrations' is a Plan of the Yeaman's Estate drawn up in 1776 (prior to the Jefferson's acquiring ownership). At that time the Estate Formed part of the Ogilvy Antiguan interests.
At some later date it was acquired by the Goodwin family, whose descendants still live on the Island.

For those readers who are particularly interested in the Jefferson's West Indies' properties, I have included an 'Attachment' to the 'Illustrations' section of this book. This attachment lists the sources from which further information can be obtained; unfortunately it is available only through the database of the Museum of Antigua and Barbuda, St. John's, Antigua, on application to the Curator of the Museum, if visiting the Island.

CHAPTER
XII

Involvement in the Development
of the Harbour

*Even before the arrival in Whitehaven of Robert
(1) Jefferson, in fact almost a century before the
Jefferson family started their business dealings in
the town, Whitehaven boasted a Shipping Fleet of
more than Seventy vessels. Sir John Lowther, an
astute businessman, had been mainly responsible
for the investment in shipping. Around 1690 he
imported craftsmen into the town, many
specialists in shipbuilding. At that time, he had
realised the value of imports as being of the
utmost benefit to the town and its economy and
was instrumental in encouraging the importation
of Tobacco from Virginia, then a British Colony
(like its counterpart, the* **Commonwealth of
Massachusetts).**

*In 1783 a magazine (The Political Magazine and
Parliamentary, Naval, Military and Literary
Journal) supplied figures indicating the tonnage
of English and Foreign ships cleared from the
five principal ports of England. These five were
listed as: London, Whitehaven*, Liverpool,
Newcastle and Bristol. In terms of tonnage,*

Whitehaven came second only to the Port of London.

(* Whitehaven's figures probably included those of tonnages from Workington, Maryport, Harrington and Parton as West Cumberland was treated as one unit.)

Until the start of the Tobacco trade, Whitehaven was trading predominantly in coal, of a recognised fine quality. Much of the coal was exported to Dublin where there was a high demand. At the time of this expansion of trade, Sir John Lowther was embarking on the genesis of Whitehaven's shipbuilding industry, as mentioned above. This created a rapid expansion in the population of the town which doubled in size over twenty two years (1693-1715).

The first import of Tobacco arrived in Whitehaven in about 1675, a trade which was to continue most profitably for well over a century.

Some well-known Whitehaven families were fore-runners in the Tobacco trade, among them being the Gales (George Gale was to marry Lucinda Mildred Washington, a Widow, and cousin of George Washington, the first President of the United States). The names of others, the Fletchers of Cockermouth and the Lutwidges (the Lutwidge Arms at Holmrook) abound in local history annals. Fletcher Christian of the 'Bounty' notoriety was kin to the Fletchers.

Whitehaven's grid pattern of streets, copied elsewhere, in the New World as well as in England, was first laid down by Sir John Lowther early in the Eighteenth century. He had stipulated that all buildings on the main streets should be three storeys high and visual evidence of that is still apparent today, on these Streets (Lowther, King, Scotch, Irish, and Duke). George Street, once a main street of the town, has been irreparably altered, for the worse.

A considerable amount of information on the growth of Whitehaven, its industries, including its most important ones of coal mining and shipbuilding from the earliest days until the mid-Nineteen-Sixties, can be found in 'A Short History of Whitehaven' by the well-respected Historian and Borough Librarian, the late Daniel Hay, listed in the Selective Bibliography of this book.

The outward journey to the 'New World' was undertaken carrying emigrants and building materials and other items required by the new settlers. Whitehaven, at that time, was one of the few ports in England licensed to import Tobacco. It had its own Customs Officer, responsible for the coastline between Maryport and Ravenglass. The Act of Union between England and Scotland

In 1707 almost 'scuppered' this most profitable business as a trade war ensued between Glasgow and Whitehaven. This culminated in an enquiry in the House of Commons over allegations that Glasgow was defrauding the Customs and Excise of Duty. Paradoxically, initially, the transport of Tobacco from Virginia to Glasgow was carried in Whitehaven vessels. The cost of the Tobacco delivered to Glasgow was higher than that delivered in Whitehaven by some 10/- to 20/- per ton (50p - £1.00 in today's currency); yet Glasgow Merchants could sell their stocks **in Cumberland** at a couple of pence less than Whitehaven's Tobacco Merchants. The Commons Select Committee enquiring into the dispute eventually ruled in favour of the Whitehaven Merchants but, by then, the Glasgow Merchants had an inexorable grip on the trade and the bulk of it eventually passed to Glasgow. The deciding factor was The American War of Independence (1775-1783) which sounded the death knell of the once lucrative Virginia/England tobacco trade. It has been estimated that Whitehaven Merchants lost about one hundred vessels during this War. Most of these were interned by the Americans whilst loading in port and some were apparently used by the Americans as 'blockships', to bar entry to American ports by Raiders from the British Navy. They were scuttled and so lost to their owners.

This squabble would more or less coincide with Robert (1's) arrival in Whitehaven, in the early Eighteenth century, probably circa 1725, when the tobacco trade was still highly profitable

His arrival marked the beginning of the Jefferson family's involvement in the Development of Whitehaven Harbour and the Trade arising from this development.

WHITEHAVEN HARBOUR
AND
THE BOARD OF TRUSTEES

A Board of Trustees of Whitehaven Harbour had been formed in the late Eighteenth century. As Wines and Spirits Merchants Jefferson's had been almost the last overseas merchants to be represented on the Harbour's Board of Trustees, Henry (1) having joined the Board during the 1790s. The character of the Board remained unchanged throughout the early Nineteenth century. Traders, Manufacturers, Wines and Spirits Merchants, Rope Makers, Bankers, Solicitors, Doctors and Clergymen were all represented on the Board over the years as can be seen by the following names and professions: Lawyers Knuckley and Garforth, a Doctor Dixon, Bankers Hamilton and Sargeant, Clergymen The Reverends Huddleston and Milner; and several Manufacturers and Tradesman including Messrs

Thomas Hartley (Ropemakers), William Miller (Tannery Owner) and Messrs Benn and Hogarth, the latter being Tradesmen in the town.

All the above men were well known in Whitehaven and their standing was such that they had a major impact on the development of the town, as well as being leading lights on the social scene. Nonetheless, despite the Board's important standing in the community and the status of the Board members, the centre of power lay with Lord Lonsdale, who as Lord of the Manor exercised considerable influence over the decisions of the Board of trustees. This made the Board's tasks quite onerous. There was to be little alteration to this state of affairs until the mid-Nineteenth century. By then the importance of Whitehaven as a major English port had waned considerably, for various reasons, the main one adversely affecting trade being the burgeoning importance of Liverpool, with its larger area, greater shipbuilding facilities, ability to handle import and distribute bulk cargoes and supplies more quickly and efficiently. Added to this was Liverpool's geographical proximity to the main markets. There were other important factors, one probably being the shallow draught at Whitehaven's harbour-mouth, which militated against its continuance as an important English port, by preventing increasingly larger-built vessels from entering the harbour.

Although we are not directly concerned with such events in this book, the above details are included to emphasise the Jefferson family's involvement in the business affairs of the town. Although the firm was not the originator of imports of wines and spirits, they quickly became one of the town's most important importers. During this period the importation of wines and spirits added significantly to the revenue accrued by the town from harbour dues. Wines and Brandy had been imported from Bordeaux in France since the late Seventeenth century and continued as high volume trade more or less steadily for more than forty years, this period coinciding with Henry (1) Jefferson (1750-1827), formerly a Master Mariner, establishing himself in business as a Wines and Spirits Merchant in 1785, following the death of his Father in 1779. By far the most important customer was Sir James Lowther who maintained large wine cellars at his homes in Whitehaven and Lowther, near Penrith.

In 1839 Henry (2) Jefferson proposed that a Steam Tug should be purchased, to tow ships in and out of Whitehaven harbour. This would replace the manual work until then carried out by rowing boats manned by ships' crews, at the same time producing Revenue for the Harbour Board. However, the Trustees decided that they did not have the power to place an order for such a vessel. Consequently, Henry (2), in collaboration with several other town notables, including one Richard Barker, formed a Company and purchased the 'Prince Albert', a Paddle Steamer, which was placed in service in 1840. One condition made by Jefferson and his partners was that this vessel would not be liable to harbour dues and charges and this proviso was accepted by the Trustees.

Initially the venture was not a success as the crews involved in the old 'manual' system were resistant to change as well as to the charges applied by the new Company. One peculiarity of the new procedure was that some of those who had previously welcomed and supported the change from manual labour to steam towing switched support back to the old system. This attitude resulted in the Company's failing in this venture and the Steamer was sold to the Trustees who, contrary to their previous misgivings, had, by then, become converted to the idea. By 1851 the 'Prince Albert' had become a regular feature of the port's activities. The use of the tug eventually became so successful that the Trustees purchased a second vessel, the Ajax, which entered into service in October 1858.

In 1868 the 'Prince Albert' was sold by Public auction for the trifling sum of £170.00, it having become beyond economic repair.

CHAPTER
XIII

Family involvement with the Military: Volunteer movements, including the Westmorland and Cumberland Yeomanry

The military commitments of the Jefferson family were established in 1809 when Robert (2) Jefferson obtained a commission on a part-time volunteer basis. This was a time of much tension between England and France – the era of Napoleon Bonaparte – when Militias throughout the country were either being created or their establishments (numbers of personnel) increased, in order to repel any possible invasion of England by the French. In 1811 Robert was gazetted a Lieutenant in the Field Artillery of the Whitehaven Militia. One can make a comparison with the present day Territorial Army. By 1813 he had attained the rank of Captain in the Militia.

Henry (3) Jefferson (1823-1896), of Springfield, near Bigrigg, Whitehaven, was involved in the early days of the 'Volunteer' movement, as had been his Father (Robert (2)(1785-1848) during the Napoleonic era.

Political considerations in the early Nineteenth century led to cutbacks in the Militia in 1827.

Presumably, these cuts arose from two considerations: the first being the defeat of Napoleon at Waterloo in 1815 which secured the security of England for a hoped for indefinite period; the second being the obvious financial savings achieved by having a reduced defence capability. This policy was reversed in the mid-Nineteenth century, through a Government circular dated 12th May 1859, sent to Lords Lieutenants of the Counties, authorising them to raise Volunteer Corps (The Yeomanry and Volunteer Consolidation Act 1804 was used as the means of this form of virtual conscription) for the defence of the Realm. The Crimean War (1854-56) had not long ended so one can only conjecture whom it was that the Government contemplated as a possible or imminent enemy.

Henry (3) was commissioned as the first Captain of the Egremont Rifles, being gazetted on 3rd July 1860 at the age of thirty-three years.

Although he was of age at the time of the Crimea War (1854-56) Henry was not called upon to serve in that campaign, although several members of the Westmorland & Cumberland Yeomanry (see below) enlisted in various Regiments which were sent to the Crimea. Two of these men actually took part in the famous (or infamous) Charge of the Light Brigade, one of them being killed in that action.

The Westmorland and Cumberland Yeomanry had been raised in October 1819, following the establishment of similar units throughout England. The reason for the creation of such bodies was the fear of the government that civil unrest could destabilise the population in the absence of a sufficiently number of police. They could therefore be used in aid of the civil power. In those days there was a certain amount of civil unrest such as strikes and occasionally, armed rebellion, because of constitutional changes in the way the country was governed. In fact similar Yeomanry Cavalry had existed since 1794 when there was a real threat of invasion by the French under Napoleon Bonaparte and they had been set up for that specific purpose.

Appointments as Officers in the C & W Yeomanry were made on the recommendation of the Lord Lieutenant of the County and consisted of local Gentlemen, well known in the County. It was normal practice to appoint a gentleman resident in the neighbourhood in which a Troop was raised. The 'other ranks' consisted of tenant farmers and landholders who had to provide their own mounts. The Government provided the necessary arms and ammunition to all. Militia service obliged members to serve for 28 days a year which was spent on training.

Henry (3) wrote to several Landowners in 1862, including Lord Leconfield (the 'Lord of the

Manor') requesting their financial help in supporting the Militia's costs. Cannily, he explained the advantages of having Militia trained men in their employment: the virtues of obedience, punctuality, discipline, 'decency' and ability to mix with other social classes, were stressed. These virtues still obtain in today's world when an Employer can consider hiring ex-Military personnel.

*The 10th Cumberland Rifle Volunteer Corps Cash Book 1860-1863 is still in the records of the family business (**vide**: 'The Rum Story' Exhibition.)*

The first Westmorland and Cumberland Yeomanry Units (originally 'Westmorland' only until 1843 when the title was changed to include Cumberland) was commanded by the Hon. Cecil Lowther. He had seen active service in regular army units and had fought in the Peninsula War.

Six troops were raised initially, at Appleby (Westmorland); Dalemain, Edenhall and Shap (all in the Penrith area); and Kendal and Milnthorpe, South Cumberland. The Whitehaven Troop was raised in 1896.

Yeomanry service obliged members to carry out 10 days' training each year; this included an annual exercise in which all the County's troops took part.

Two members of the family were militarily involved in the Yeomanry in the late 19th century.

Robert (5) Jefferson (1857-1942), the eldest son of the above Henry (3), had held a commission in the Westmorland & Cumberland Yeomanry since 1885, serving in the Lowther (Shap) Troop. The Notice of his appointment appeared in the 'London Gazette' of 19th March 1886 (sic), as follows:

'Robert Jefferson, Gentleman, to be Lieutenant (Supernumerary) posted to Lowther Troop'.

Robert (5) lived at Rosehill, Whitehaven, and, in 1894, married Miss Constance Lumb (or Lamb?), the daughter of a Mr Lumb (Lamb) of Homewood, Whitehaven. Subsequent to the marriage they raised two children.

On 10th May 1896, Robert (5) was transferred from Lowther Troop and was appointed to the command of the newly formed 'Whitehaven' Troop of the Yeomanry. On 7th April 1897 he was promoted to the rank of Captain and Troop Commander. He retired from the Yeomanry in 1901 in the rank of Honorary Major (promoted on 27th April 1901) in which rank he retired, without seeing active service. The Boer War had started in 1900 and the W & C Yeomanry saw much action in that campaign.

A photograph of Robert appear in the Appendices to this book.

Lieutenant Joseph Hugh Jefferson (1859-1920), known as 'Hugh', was the younger brother of Robert (5). He lived at St. Helens, Cockermouth and, in 1888, married the only daughter of Mr Dixon, Rheda, Frizington, near Whitehaven. They had two children.

The 'London Gazette' of 8th July 1891, published the following Bulletin: 'Westmorland and Cumberland Yeomanry Cavalry, Joseph Hugh Jefferson, Gentleman, to be 2nd Lieutenant (Supernumerary).

On 10th May 1896, Hugh was posted to the newly formed 'Whitehaven' Troop, as Subaltern, serving under his elder brother Robert (above). Hugh was transferred to the Carlisle Troop in the rank of Captain on 5th May 1898.

A photograph of Hugh also appears in the Appendices Section.

*A problem arose in 1900, when the Manager of Jefferson's Wines and Spirits business (by then known as 'R. & H. Jefferson) fell ill. This situation made it impossible for **both** the brothers (Robert and Hugh) to attend for training simultaneously, so they took it in turns to report* *for duty. A similar situation arose the following year. This culminated in Robert's resignation; Hugh's resignation from the Yeomanry followed in June 1901. The reasons put forward were that it was on account of their both being required to attend to the family business.*

Robert (5's) son, Henry (4) also served with the Westmorland and Cumberland Yeomanry Cavalry and later, during the First World War, with the 5th Dragoon Guards. He was wounded whilst on active service and information to this effect is posted on the St. Bees School Roll of Honour Board, where he had been educated. Henry (4) later served post-war in the British army of Occupation of the Rhine.

CHAPTER
XIV

Local Churches connected
with the Jefferson Family

St. Nicholas Church, Lowther Street, Whitehaven:

*Some records of the Jefferson family state that at least one member was interred in St. Nicholas Churchyard. This is patently incorrect. One source, usually quite accurate in its reporting, states that **Thomas,** first-born child of **Robert (1)** was buried at St. Nicholas's, beside the bodies of three infants who had been buried prior to Thomas's death. In fact, the records of The Holy Trinity Church, Scotch Street, Whitehaven, clearly show that Thomas died on $2^{nd.}$ January 1770, at the age of twenty-one and was interred alongside three infants, and was accurately reported. The three infants referred to were most likely Thomas's three younger siblings who had pre-deceased him. They were John: (born 1757 and died at nine months' of age); Daniel: (born 1758 who died at only four weeks old); and Mary: (born in 1759 and died in 1762.)*

The writer recently visited the Churchyard of St. Nicholas to examine the Headstones still in place. No trace of any 'Jefferson' could be found. Nevertheless it is still possible, but unlikely that one or more members of the family could be buried there, or may have even worshipped at St. Nicholas Church. The lettering on those Headstones remaining is almost obliterated through the passage of time and the nature of the stonework, many being carved from sandstone which has eroded.

The Holy Trinity Church, Scotch Street, Whitehaven:

Some of the Jefferson's found their last resting place in this Churchyard. Although it was plain on the outside the Church was elaborate and attractive within. Sadly the Church was declared unsafe over fifty years ago, being demolished in 1949. The Churchyard was converted into a garden of rest and the Headstones were arranged around the walls of the Churchyard and also in a horizontal position in the far section of the Yard. Again, most of the lettering on many Headstones has been destroyed by the ravages of the weather and no trace of any members of the Jefferson family could be found.

The following principal members of the family are interred in this Churchyard:

Robert (1)   Died 18th. October 1779; buried on 21st. October 1779 (also his wife Martha who died on 6th. January 1783**)**

Henry (1)   Died 13th. December 1827 (also his wife Ann(e) who died on 20th. May 1820)

St. John's, Bigrigg:

On 8th August 1880, Henry (3), ceded part of the Springfield property to the Church Commissioners. The land was given for the purpose of erecting a Church on the property. It was passed to William Edmund Strickland, Rector of Egremont '**to erect additional church for the parish at or near Bigrigg to Egremont district Church of St. John............**' This was erected on part of field 100 (see first Edition of Ordnance Survey Map). '**containing front to the highway leading from Whitehaven to Egremont 135 feet 5 inches and at the back thereof 139 feet and in breadth at the north end and 81 feet 5 inches at the south end 84 feet 5 inches or thereabouts.........for a Church of England Church and for no other purpose whatsoever.**'

The Church was duly built and was consecrated as a Chapel-of-ease in 1880 and was built to hold 250 worshippers. The Jefferson's also provided two stained glass windows, one behind the font and one behind the altar. The front window was *erected by Mary Watts Jefferson (wife of Henry (3)) in 'dutiful memory of her parents'. The Chancel window bears the inscription 'In Honour of Christ crucified, and in loving memory of Henry Jefferson of Springfield who died November 27th. 1896 aged 77 years, this window is dedicated.'*

The Jefferson's of Springfield had previously dedicated a window and a commemorative plaque in St. Mary and St. Michael's, the parish church, in Egremont. Of these there is now no trace whatsoever.

Robert (5) *Died on 31st. May 1942 and buried in Egremont Cemetery on 4th. June 1942.*

St.Mary and St.Michael's, Egremont:

Robert (2) *Died 24th. September 1848. A memorial stone was placed in the South transept of the Church but this Church was demolished in 1883 and a new Church erected in its place. The memorial stone, which also bore the name of Robert's wife Elizabeth (who lived for three year's after Robert's death), has not been found. The Rector of the Church has no record of the whereabouts of this stone and there are no references to the Jefferson family anywhere, either inside the Church or in the Churchyard.*

Henry (3)   Died on 27th. November 1896 and was interred in the family vault. Although the Churchyard had been closed in the 1860s and all interments had been removed to the new Churchyard on the outskirts of Egremont, there was a special dispensation at Henry's request, for him to be buried in the family vault. Henry had reserved this right at the time of the Churchyard's closure.

Peculiarly there is no trace of the location of this family Vault. The Rector of the Church has no knowledge and advised the writer that there are no signs of any vaults below the floor coverings of the Church.

St. Bees Priory:

Henry (2)   Died on 19th. July 1877 and buried on 23rd. July 1877. There is a full
report on Henry's funeral in Chapter IV.

There is a Memorial tablet commemorating Henry Jefferson (1800-1877)
and his wife Ann (1799-1854) in the Priory.

Robert (5)   Died on 31st. May 1942 and interred in Egremont Cemetery, following a service at St. John's Church, Bigrigg.

NOTES:

In 1812 Henry (1) Jefferson gave a subscription of 10/- (or a half-guinea – 10/6d.?) towards the cost of a new Chandelier for The Holy Trinity Church. The total cost of the Chandelier was £44.7.2d. There is reference to this in a 'History of The Holy Trinity Church 1715-1949'; Plate 70; Author: Ann Dick, 1991)

The Register of Headstones in the graveyard of The Holy Trinity Church supplies the following information:

Died

Jefferson	Henry (Merchant)
13/12/1827: **Henry (1)** - age 77	
	Ann (wife of above)
20/05/1820 - age 56	
	Ann (daughter of above)
20/12/1820 - age 38	
	Elizabeth (" " ")
21/03/1826 - age 32	
	Margaret (" " ")
26/11/1828 - age 27	
	Thomas (son of above). Died in Valparaiso on 12/06/1836 at the age of 33 years

Jefferson family marriages recorded at The Holy Trinity Church between 1715 and 1837:

Ann; Charlotte; Daniel; Eleanor: Elizabeth; George; Hannah; Henry; Jane; Martha; Mary; Nathaniel; Robert; Sarah; Tamara; Thomas; William.

There are no indications as to which branch(es) of the Jefferson the above relate. One can make comparisons with the Jefferson Family Tree in the Appendices of this book.

Henry (2)   Baptised at Holy Trinity on $19^{th.}$ January 1801
Henry (3)   Baptised at Holy Trinity Church on $3^{rd.}$ December 1837*

*This baptism is recorded in the Parish Records of Holy Trinity Church for the period 1800-1837. It could only possibly refer to **Henry (3)** as Henry (1) had died in 1827 and Henry (2's) baptism is shown above. Henry (4) was only born in 1896. Therefore, Henry (3) must have been Fourteen years of age at the time of his baptism, having been born in 1823!

There are also some short references to the Jefferson Family in an Appendix to this Book.

There is a photograph of Bigrigg Church (St.John's) in the 'Illustrations' of this Book.

Also buried in Egremont Cemetery:

Henry (4) The last Male in the Family hierarchy and the last Henry Jefferson to run the family business.

Born: 1896

Died: 1st June 1979

Henry was buried in Egremont Cemetery and there is a Headstone at the site of his grave.
He married Elizabeth Wadham in 1927.

Because of the lack of family records (as mentioned elsewhere) nothing of personal interest could be recorded.

CHAPTER
XV

Involvement in Politics

The Jefferson family became involved in local politics more or less as a matter of course and this involvement resulted in some acrimony between Henry (2) and the Second Earl of Lonsdale.

In 1832, an election was held for the Harbour Board of Trustees. These elections were held every three years and Robert (2) Jefferson (1785-1848) was one of those appointed to the Board. Because of the Reform Act of 1832 Whitehaven, previously not having had its own representation in Parliament, became a separate constituency. In the General Election which followed this reform, a Tory candidate, Matthias Attwood, was sponsored by Robert (2).

Sir William Lowther, FRS, became the Second Earl of Lonsdale in 1844, following the death of his Father. There must have been a hereditary breakdown as the First Earl had been given the acronym 'William the Good'; his son, however, was soon awarded the dubious title of 'William the Bad' as he was much less of a philanthropist. Whereas his Father had carried out work for the benefit f the community, including financing the

building, in 1808, of Whitehaven's first
subscription Library, public benefaction was not
apparently the first of the Second Earl's
priorities.   Nevertheless, he was largely
responsible for the extension of the Railway Line
to Whitehaven (between 1845 and 1847) where,
previously, it had ceased at Maryport.*   The
Second Earl had considerable experience in
National Government, with a total of 33 years as
a Tory MP, including a stint as Postmaster
General, before being raised to the House of
Lords. His experience, allied to his vast fortune
and considerable capabilities as a businessman,
had given him great power and influence in the
Tory Party.

In 1846 the Conservative (Tory) Government led
by Sir Robert Peel, the Prime Minister, repealed
The Corn Laws, an act that aroused the fury of
many wealthy land-owners, and others with
vested interested in the continuation of these
Laws. In common with others throughout the
country, many leading figures reviewed their
allegiances and Whitehaven was no exception,
Henry (2) being one of those who changed his
political affiliation.   Formerly a Tory, he
assumed the leadership of the Whig group and
this was the direct cause of a schism in 1850
between Henry (2) and William 'The Bad'
(Lonsdale), involving the Whitehaven Harbour
Trustees.   Henry (2) had previously been a
supporter of the Lowther (Lonsdale) family.

There was a blatant attempt to prevent voters from exercising their only recently won right to vote, an affair now secret and not on Public Hustings. The only Polling Station in the town was located in the Old Records office on Lowther Street (now the site of Whitehaven's General Post Office) and Henry (2) was instrumental in arranging the blocking of the intersections of Lowther Street/Scotch Street and Lowther Street/Queen Street (the Records Office lying in between these two points). The barricades remained in place for a whole week. Only those Voters favourable to Henry (2) were allowed through to register their votes as Whig supporters 'manned the barricades' and blocked their rivals' passage to the Polling Station. Henry (2) easily topped the poll and, despite protests to the Electoral Authority from William (the Second Earl), the result of the Vote was allowed to stand and Henry (2) was declared the winner for the Whig Party which formed the majority of the elected Town and Harbour Trustees. This infuriated the Second Earl. Thereafter, additional Polling Stations were erected as and when needed, to prevent any recurrence of this blatantly unscrupulous behaviour.

Henry (2's) success was short-lived however. William installed a relative, the Reverend Henry Lowther, as Chairman of the Board of Trustees and he stymied any attempt by Henry (2) and his associates to push through any of their proposals

Having failed to secure re-election in 1853 and 1856, Henry (2) managed to secure election as a Trustee for the St. Nicholas ward at their tri-annual elections of 1859.

*This work was executed by his friend George Stephenson (of 'Rocket' fame), who was the world's First Railwayman.

CHAPTER
XVI

Residential Property Ownership

Between them, the Jefferson family owned (or leased*) a number of select residential properties in the Whitehaven area.

Marlborough Street:

*The Founder of the Jefferson Dynasty, **Robert (1) (1704-1779)**, lived in one of the then large Merchants' Houses in this street which adjoined the Harbour, near the Lime (New) Tongue. Nothing is known about this Dwelling, and the properties on Marlborough Street, which had deteriorated badly, were demolished in the 1960s during a slum clearance and re-housing scheme.*

Nevertheless, there is an illustration of the house of Thomas Hartley, Merchant (and Ropemaker) in the Town's Record Office (Archives), which gives an accurate indication of the quality of the property. Hartley's house was substantially built, on three storeys, at the end of the street and facing the Lime (New Tongue). Adjoining houses seem to be of similar type and are an indication of the status of the occupants.

The location would be ideal for Robert to follow his occupation as a Master Mariner.

Robert died at his Marlborough Street home.

4 Cross Street:

Henry (1) (1750-1827), *the actual Founder of the family business, initially lived at an address in Queen Street but re-located to 4 Cross Street on his marriage to Ann(e) Tweedie, in Antigua in 1780.*

The House still stands but with no distinguishing feature, nor any commemorative plaque, as is sometimes erected as a tribute to prominent citizens of the town.

The houses on Cross Street, a short street, are all of a type; they would have been large and imposing at the time of their erection, and were substantially built.

Henry died at this address; yet his wife, Ann(e) died at an address given as Lowther Street. It may be that she was residing at the Jefferson family's premises in Lowther Street but that is unlikely as it was wholly a place of business.

Keekle Grove: * *(leased)*

This Mansion was one of the older houses on the outskirts of Cleator Moor. Standing near the banks of the Keekle River, facing and close to Whinney Hill, it commanded fine views of Dent and the Ennerdale Fells. There is no record of the date the Mansion was built, but examination of the stonework in the early Nineteenth century indicated considerable antiquity.

*It first came to prominence in the early Nineteenth century when it was advertised 'To Let' by the owner. Several tenants occupied it from 1804 until it passed into the hands of **Robert (2) Jefferson** prior to 1839, before his purchase of Springfield.*

The description of the Mansion is interesting and it appears to have been a most delightful residence, described thus in 1804 :

"Beautiful Mansion, Plantations, Shrubberies, Gardens, Stable and Coachhouse. Two and a half miles from Whitehaven. The property of Charles Deane, Esq. Optional, twenty acres of good land in a high state of cultivation. The present tenant is Mr. Nicholson. Apply to Mr. John Litt, Nether End."

The (optional) land was subsequently let to the tenants of Montreal Farm, Cleator Moor.

*Following the departure of Robert (2), Keekle Grove was tenanted by a member of the Key family (Samuel Key was Lord of the Manor of Fulford, York.) To show how interwoven were the local dynasties, it is interesting to note that a son of Samuel Key, also named Samuel, married, in 1839, Harriet, daughter of William Lumb, J.P., D.L., of Meadow House, Whitehaven. Most likely, this William Lumb was a forebear of the Mr. Lumb (Lamb?) of Homewood, Whitehaven, whose daughter, Constance, married **Robert (5)** Jefferson in 1894.*

However, on the death of the Owner, Charles Deane, the property came under the jurisdiction of his nephew and executor, Anthony Parkin of Sharrow Bay, near Ullswater. Life interest in the Estate was granted to Charles Deane's two sisters during their lifetime, after which ownership passed to Anthony Parkin. Other members of the Parkin family later occupied the property and then came a succession of non-family tenants, of a variety of occupations. At some time after 1897 it was divided into two properties and then the property faded from the records.

There appear to have been numerous alterations to Keekle House, with some drastic alterations currently ongoing. It is totally unrecognisable from the description of 1804. The house stands adjacent to the B 5295, only a few hundred yards from the Keekle Viaduct.

Springfield House:

In 1841 **Robert (2) (1785-1848)** *completed the purchase of Springfield House. This property had belonged to Sir John Ponsonby and came up for sale following his death.*

Robert had already leased Springfield two years earlier, in 1839, a signatory being Robert's eldest son, **Henry (3).**

Springfield is located on the outskirts of Bigrigg, a village less than three miles from Whitehaven on the A 595 road to Egremont. A description given in the Cumberland Pacquet of 10$^{th.}$ May 1814 says:

"To be sold in Public Sale on Friday the 1$^{st.}$ day of July next, 1814, at the Golden Lion Whitehaven "....The freehold Estate of Springfield....the Mansion House, gardens, stables, coachhouse and offices, being all in complete repair and fit for the immediate reception of a Gentleman's family." All the appurtenances therefore for someone of high social standing in the district.

Surviving documents list the original property as dating from 1738.

There is a lodge at the entrance to the property, near the main road (this was also purchased by Robert at the time of his acquisition of Springfield.) Its outward appearance seems to have changed little from the time it was built. A photograph of the Lodge can also be found in the 'Illustrations' section. At the time of Robert's occupation this house was occupied by the family's butler.

*In the British Census of 1871, during occupation of Springfield by Robert's eldest son, **Henry (3)** which he had inherited from his Father, the servants living on the property were listed as:*

Coachman, Cook, Housemaid, Children's Nurse, Kitchenmaid and Undernurse.

In 1881 the staff comprised of:

Laundrymaid, Housemaid, Underhousemaid, Kitchenmaid, Coachman and Groom.

In those days of long-service by servants with a particular family, there was apparently quite a high turnover of staff as only one member was listed on consecutive Census Returns of 1861 and 1871. A Footman, one William Johnston, who appeared in the 1861 Census also appeared in the Census for 1871 as 'Butler'; but, by 1881 he too had disappeared from the scene.

*When **Henry (3)** died in 1896, the contents of Springfield were valued at under £1,000.00, an extremely small amount even at that time. This valuation included all the 'household furniture, horses, harness, coaches and other effects'. Surprisingly, a pig in the outside yard was also included as were ten dozen flowerpots. The Library listed books by well-known Authors of the time, including Boswell's Life of Dr. Johnson, Charles Dickens (nineteen volumes), Sir Walter Scott (18 volumes of the 'Waverley Novels').*

The size of Springfield can be judged by the rooms listed:

Five Bedrooms, two with Dressing Rooms, plus a Nursery; added to which are rooms for the housemaids, cooks, kitchenmaids and butler (the 'butler's pantry where the butler would while away his time when not required by his Employer; time usually spent cleaning and checking the family silver, etc.).

In 1880, part of the property was given to the Rector of Egremont (see Chapter XIV).

In the Jefferson family property passed through the male line. On Robert's death, a proviso in his *will was that his Widow, Elizabeth, be granted the use of the house and its contents during her lifetime, **provided she did not remarry**. She was also granted an Annuity of £500.00 per annum. Unfortunately Elizabeth lived for only three years after Robert's death.*

***Henry (3)** continued to live at the property from the time of his inheritance until his death.*

The Jefferson family continued to live at Springfield until the property was sold in 1949.

Springfield is now subdivided into several self-contained units and no longer possesses the grandeur of its former days. The grounds, although reasonably well kept, can best be described as 'orderly'; certainly there are no signs of the normal formal grounds one could reasonably expect in a Mansion.

A photograph of the House as it looks in the year 2005 can be found in the 'Illustrations' Section of this book.

An interesting footnote to the history of Springfield is that, in papers found after Henry (3's) death in 1896, a list of Servants and their pay had been compiled, viz:

SERVANTS

			£	s	d
Gray	Coachman	Cottage free	4	8	0*
Jeffrey	Butler	Lives in House	3	6	8*
Jackson	Gardener	Cottage free	4	8	0*
Benson	Boy	Lives out		12	0*
Anderson	Cook	House servant	7	10	0+
Johnston	Kitchenmaid	House servant	3	0	0+
Gibson	Housemaid	House servant	5	10	0+
Little	Underhouse-Maid	House Servant	4	0	0+
Black	Laundrymaid	Lodge Free		15	0#

*   Per Month
\+   Per Quarter
\#   Per Fortnight

For some reason the Laundrymaid is noted as living in the Lodge, normally the Butler's residence

Note: In today's money these sums are pittances. Nevertheless, at the end of the 19th century, to be in regular employment, with free accommodation provided, was most acceptable.

Rosehill:

Robert (5)(1857-1942) lived at Rosehill, on the outskirts of Whitehaven, near Low Moresby, until *he inherited **Springfield**. This house survives to this day and is a spacious and attractive Gentleman's residence, with limited grounds.*

Rothersyke House:

Rothersyke House is probably the most interesting dwelling in the family history, largely because, today, it remains substantially unaltered, judging from its exterior appearance anyway.

***Henry (2) (1800-1877)** built Rothersyke, near Egremont, some time between 1847 (when it was not listed in local records) and the Census of 1851. At that time he describes himself as a 'JP and West India Merchant'. Also listed as residents on the property in that year are his wife and four children, plus seven other people. (See the Family Tree for the total number of children born to Henry and his wife Ann Jefferson (nee Davidson.)   The seven other persons are identified in the records as being four house servants and two farm servants and one 'scholar', the latter presumably a child of one of the farm servants.*

It is described in the 1858 Post Office Directory as a 'handsome modern stone mansion'.

*The Jefferson family lived in the house until 1902 – **Henry (2)** being followed in line of succession by his son **Robert (3) (1826-1902).***

One very unfortunate aspect of the family's association with Rothersyke is that Robert remained a bachelor and, following his death, the property was sold, there being no heirs to inherit it (see below.) The buyer was Lord Leconfield.

A clause in Henry (2's) will, proved in 1877, had expressly specified that Robert had free use of the House and Lands of Rothersyke (together with 'the meadow at St. Bees') during his lifetime, but, if he died 'without issue' (i.e. no heirs), then the Trustees must sell the property, which is what happened.

When the property was sold in 1903, its description was as follows:

'Mansion House and grounds, farmhouse, farm buildings, two cottages, land, etc. containing together 128 acres 3 roods* and 19.160 perches* The catalogue for the sale listed the bedrooms as numbering ten, excluding the servants' quarters.

*(rood: one quarter of an acre
   perch: a measure of land equal to a quarter of a chain approximately 51/2 yards.)

The Farm listed in the sale was owned by the Jefferson family. It pre-dated Henry's building of the House but formed part of the Estate. The Farm was also sold to Lord Leconfield on 4th. March 1903 together with the House and other property.

The tenant of the farm, at the time of Robert (3's) death was one James Allonby and he was left a legacy of £50.00, a not inconsiderable sum in those days. Allonby had served as Bailiff for Robert.

At the farm sale R & H Jefferson provided 12 gallons of 'Old Highland' whisky, 3 gallons of choice Jamaica Rum and 21/2 dozen Schweppes soda water. Total price was £16.19.0d. It must have been thirsty work or else very cold on that day (March) perhaps encouraging the potential buyers to remain at the sale.

At Robert's death the wages bill for the servants showed that £47.15.0d was owed to household servants and £58.6.0d for Hind# and farm servants.

*(****Hind****: a skilled farm worker (Scottish term)*

The sale of furniture, silver plate and plated goods, china, pictures, glass, carpets, bed and table linen, wines and other effects ran to 964 lots and took place over four days (10-13 March

1903.) A point of interest is that, relating to the valuation carried out at Springfield following the death of Henry (3) when eighteen volumes of Sir Walter Scott's 'Waverley' novels were listed in the inventory, another thirty-five by the same Author were included in the Rothersyke Sale.

A recent photograph of the house is shown in the 'Illustrations' to this book. Its appearance is very pleasant but the grounds surrounding the property are in a very poor state, much run down and overgrown. In its day it must have been a charming, rustic retreat for a Country Squire or successful Merchant. For some time, in recent years, it was used as a Retirement Home and it is situated in a very quiet, rural part of West Cumbria, quite close to Egremont.

St Helens, Cockermouth:

***Joseph Hugh Jefferson**, about whom little has been recorded, other than his Sporting and Military activities, lived at this address during his marriage to Elizabeth Ann Dixon, late of Rheda, Frizington.*

Nothing is known about this house; most likely it was one of the properties in St. Helens Street, Cockermouth, now mainly commercially owned.

One can still discern faint signs that there were once substantially built and imposing residences in this street. It is again apparent that Robert (5) kept a somewhat 'low profile' when it came to his private affairs as no records exist of this house nor other than slight reference to it.

Hensingham House:

*The only information about this residence is that **Henry (2)** lived there for a while after moving from an address in Lowther Street in about 1837. They remained at Hensingham until Henry built Rothersyke in the late 1840s.*

The House still exists and does not appear to have been substantially changed on the exterior except for intrusions onto the grounds of properties built later. It stands adjacent to the Church at Hensingham, a building in the Early English style although built only in 1913, on a site donated by the Earl of Lonsdale.

The

JEFFERSON'S

of

WHITEHAVEN

Chapter XVII

Conclusion

It is most unfortunate that the male line of the Jefferson family ceased, following the death of Henry (4) in 1979. He had continued the business after his Father (Robert (5)) died in 1942.

Henry (4's) children, daughters Constance and Elizabeth carried on the family business after their Father's death but, for their own reasons ceased trading on 27$^{th.}$ June 1998. Even as the oldest Wines and Spirits Merchants in the Country (established in 1785) and with an excellent reputation, allied with high quality products (especially their famous Jefferson's Fine Old Rum), competition from other specialist Liquor Merchants, especially national chain outlets and the supermarkets, was slowly (and

*not so slowly) taking a stranglehold on the Wines
and Spirits market throughout the country.*

*A financial settlement was reached with the
Whitehaven Development Company which
acquired the property and all the associated
goods and chattels of the business, following
disposal of the stock. The Company received
financial support from the National Lottery and
was also part-financed by the European Regional
Development Fund. The result has become an
outstanding and permanent tourist attraction,
with numerous visitors throughout the year.*

*The new owners, Whitehaven Development
Company, embarked on a most ambitious scheme
as part of the re-generation of Whitehaven and
its Harbour, something which the Town was
urgently in need. The outcome was 'The Rum
Story', a quite fascinating Exhibition, based on
the Jefferson's involvement in the Rum Trade
with the West Indies. Sailing their own Fleet of
Ships, mainly to Antigua, they returned with
Rum, Sugar and Molasses, thus embarking on
what was to be their principal business for more
than two centuries. This history is told in the
Exhibition through the use of realistic sound
effects, dioramas and displays of numerous
artefacts and some considerable reference to
Slavery in which the Jefferson's were
emphatically not involved. The fact that the
premises retain almost all of its original features,*

including Cellars, Bonded Store, lends a truly authentic air to the Exhibition.

Very little documentary evidence however is available on the full extent of their Plantations and holdings in Antigua. What information has been made available, from sources in Antigua has contradicted both the dates and the extent of the Jefferson's Holdings on the Island and also on St. Kitt's, the neighbouring Island. The evidence available, including the contradictory material has been set out in Chapter Eleven. Readers may also refer to the Bibliography of this Book and read portions of 'From Cumberland to Cape Horn', which provides some personal details of the Jefferson's exploits. What is known however is that, at no time was the Jefferson family slave owners. It is recorded that, upon the Jefferson's acquisition of the Yeaman's Estate, all Slaves listed in the Conveyancing as part of the stock were immediately given their freedom.

Suffice it to say the earlier members of the family, especially the second and third generations - Henry (1), Robert (2) and Henry (2) were most active in this side of the business. The success of the family was of course due mainly to Robert (1) Jefferson, the Master Mariner, from Aikton, near Wigton, who began the enterprise, importing a variety of products, principally tobacco (from Virginia) into Whitehaven.

At that time the Business Premises on Lowther Street (stretching well back and abutting Chapel Street) had acquired the status of a Grade II listed building. Much of the original structure of the firm's offices was retained along with displays of family portraits and paintings, hunting trophies, etc. Ancient office equipment was also still in use at the time the firm closed, albeit alongside more modern items. The office, now forming part of 'The Rum Story', gives one quite an accurate presentation of the centuries-old business. Modern lighting has replaced the old-fashioned gas lights and fires but, entering the office, one can quickly get the sense of times past.

Given that running a business of such a diverse nature – buying, selling or chartering Vessels; maintaining crews for these; shipping and its attendant problems of weather conditions timescales, etc.; import; export; handling; bottling; barrel-making (cooperage) and assorted but necessary lesser duties, it is hard to envisage that any members of the family were able – and willing – to perform such a variety of civic duties, many honorary only, that they indeed carried out through several generations.

Of course, in those times of post-Industrial Revolution growth and Victorian values, the better-off (the 'gentry'), with minions to carry out day to day drudgery, had more time to devote themselves to 'good works' than the ordinary members of the working-classes. Nevertheless, much good work was done by members of the Jefferson clan, for the benefit of the townspeople of Whitehaven and surrounding areas. Nowadays, many people serving on Councils throughout the land do so more for pecuniary advantage than for a wish to help their fellow-men without expectation of financial reimbursement.

The time taken up with these civic duties – sitting as Magistrates, School Governors, Chairmen of various Boards, including Hospitals, must have exacted a considerable toll on the Jefferson's. It is noticeable than, in the post-war years (Second World War), their participation declined considerably. This may have been due to post-war austerity measures which affected almost everyone, a reluctance on the part of later generations to become involved in this type of honorary work, financial constraints, or an amalgam of the above.

*It is noteworthy to record that the male Jefferson's invariably made sound financial provision for the females of the family, sisters, daughters, wives, whatever generation we may enquire into. This is a most laudable example of the respect in which **all** members of the family* *were held and is a good barometer of the high quality of their breeding.*

An indication of the financial foresight shown by the Jefferson family can be found by examining the Share portfolios of several members of the family.

Robert (3) invested heavily not just in local Railway enterprises such as the Cleator and Egremont (and Workington) Junction Railway and the Maryport to Carlisle Railway, but also further afield and also internationally. Following his death in 1902, his will revealed shareholdings in the following Railway ventures:-

The Liverpool Overhead Railway; Buenos Aires Great Southern Railway Company, Caledonian Railway Company and the Midland Railway.

Henry (3) also had substantial investments as was revealed in his will, these being :-

The Furness Railway, Caledonian Railway, Nitrate Railway Co. Limited, the Rio Claro to Sao Paulo Railway Company Limited, Antofogasta Railway (Chile) and the Bolivian Railway Company Limited.

These shares were all sold by the executors.

A major drawback in compiling this short history of the Jefferson family has been the plethora of identical names such as 'Robert' and 'Henry'. This has tended to confuse other writers and I myself have found it quite a handicap when researching the family's history. In fact, even old documents dating back to the late Nineteenth and early Twentieth centuries have made errors of identification of various 'Roberts' and 'Henrys'.
I apologise if, on occasions, I may have inadvertently misled the reader.

*Another factor which has inhibited a more or less complete disclosure of Jefferson family history, is the lack of items of **personal** correspondence, photographs, etc., from the later generations of the family. These were apparently lost or permanently mislaid during the transition of the business from an operating entity to its total transformation as 'The Rum Centre'. Another unfortunate fact is that, despite the Jefferson's owning a number of ships, only one picture has been located, this being a photograph of an original oil painting of the 'British Queen'. It has been included in this book.*

Whilst this book does not purport to be a complete history of the Jefferson family, it details as much information about the family as is available from local and international research.

Brian Parnaby

Ullock   *March 2005*

Selective Bibliography

Bardgett, D.   Better By Far A
                                Cumberland
                                Hussar,
                                published 2001

Caine, C.   The Churches of
                                Whitehaven Rural
                                Deanery, A History
                                of,
                                published 1916

Caine, C.   Cleator and Cleator
                                Moor, Past and
                                Present,
                                published 1916

(Cumberland)
County Annual   1900-1904
Cumbria Record
Office, Carlisle   Parish Records of
                                Holy Trinity
                                Church,
                                Whitehaven

Hay, D.   Whitehaven,
                                an Illustrated
                                History,
                                published 1979

Hay, D.   A short History
                                of Whitehaven,
                                published 1968

Hollett, D.   From Cumberland
                                to Cape Horn,
                                published 1984

	Cumberland Pacquet, 1779
Jefferson, Elizabeth.	Personal Recollections
Rum Story Exhibition, The	Lowther Street, Whitehaven
Scott-Hindson, Brian	Whitehaven Harbour, published 1994
Whitehaven News, The	3rd December 1896; 26th July 1877 4th June 1942

THE JEFFERSON'S
of
WHITEHAVEN

APPENDIX 'A'

Vessels Owned or Chartered by
The Company

The following is a list of the Vessels owned by the Jefferson's, with a brief history of their activities:

Name	Type	Registered Tonnage	Built By/At	Date
GALE	*Snow (Brig)*	*200 tons*	*? ....,* *Whitehaven*	*1758*

Remarks:

A 'Brig' is a two-masted, square-rigged sailing vessel and a 'Snow' is actually a Brig but with an additional (Trysail) mast. Brigs were fairly common in the mid-Eighteenth century and were generally used as colliers, transporting coal from the Northern coalfields (e.g. West Cumberland) to London and other major English ports. Despite its limited tonnage, a 200-tonner was not a small vessel by the standards of the day. Notwithstanding that, transatlantic voyages in poor weather conditions must have been uncomfortable and somewhat hazardous at times. Brigs are still fairly common, even today, being used as sail-training vessels.

The 'Gale' must have been named after a member of the Gale family, well known in the town of Whitehaven where they were involved in trade as Merchants, including tobacco. The family is mainly remembered in Whitehaven for an indirect connection with George Washington, the first President of the United States of America. (Interested readers should refer to the Author's 'Notes' for details of this connection).

The 'Gale' was registered E 1 at Lloyds of London and was acquired by the Jefferson's in 1775, with Henry (1) as its new Master. It made several voyages for the Jefferson's before being sold.

Between Whitehaven - London - Virginia: 1776
London – Quebec: 1778-1779
Whitehaven – Antigua: 1781 (new owner)

The trade in Tobacco must have been thwarted, or at least interrupted, by the American War of Independence (1775-1783) which would have effectively forced any English vessels to seek trade elsewhere.

Captains:

Henry (1) Jefferson: Henry (1) assumed command of the 'Gale', the first vessel purchased by the Jefferson family, at the age of twenty-five, as co-owner with his Father, Robert (1). He had followed Robert into the same profession as Master Mariner and Merchant and, naturally, entered the Virginia trade, more fully described in Henry (1's) biography elsewhere in this book. Henry remained as Master of the 'Gale' until 1781, when the ship was sold to a Captain Parker.

Captain …….. Parker: master from 1781 (continued with same trade)

DORIS	*Brigantine*	*133 tons*	*T & J Brocklebank*	*1818*
			Whitehaven	

Remarks:

A Brigantine (Briganteen) is a two-masted sailing vessel, square-rigged on the foremast and fore-and-aft rigged on the aftermast. This type of vessel was used mainly in the late Nineteenth century. Very few are still in commission, certainly none being used for commercial purposes.

The 'Doris' was built at the Brocklebank's Shipyard. Shortly after the launch in 1818 she was sold to the Jefferson's.

The following voyages are recorded:

1819, 1820, 1821: Liverpool – Brazil
1822, 1823, 1824: Liverpool – Charleston, Virginia
1825   : Liverpool – St. Domingo (now Dominican Republic)

The Master on the above voyages was Captain John White.

On 15 April 1825 a report was received from Nassau, Bahamas, that the 'Doris' had been lost on Heneaga (approximate latitude tropic of Cancer?) on passage tp Falmouth, Cornwall. Captain John White, the Master, his crew and some of the cargo were saved but the vessel was a total loss.

THETIS	*Brigantine*	*161 tons*	*William Wilson,*	*1817*
	Rig		*Whitehaven*	

Remarks:

Also rigged as a Brigantine, but with slightly larger overall dimensions than the 'Doris'.

This vessel was purchased by Jefferson's from the Ship-Builders in 1825. Prior to then the 'Thetis' had been chartered from Wilson by the Jefferson family.

The following voyages are recorded:

Whitehaven – Antigua:	*1824*	*Whilst on Charter*	*Captain John Taylor*
Whitehaven – Antigua:	*1826*	*New owners*	*-do-*
Whiteaven – Montego Bay:	*1827*		*Captain J Robinson*
Whitehaven – Oporto:	*1828-1829*		*Captain Henry Booth Hewitt*
Whitehaven – Antigua:	*1830-1833*		*-do-*
Whitehaven – Antigua:	*1834*		*Captain Benjamin Wheelright*
Whitehaven – Antigua:	*1834-1835*		*Captain William Harper*
Liverpool – Antigua:	*1836-1837*		*-do-*

In May 1837, the 'Thetis' foundered off Cape Finisterre after striking a sunken wreck. Two passengers and one crew member were lost in this shipwreck.

In view of the number of sailings between Whitehaven and Antigua it can reasonably be presumed that the Jefferson's were fast becoming heavily involved in the shipping of goods, especially Rum, from that island to Whitehaven (and later, Liverpool) ; with shipping from other countries playing a lesser role in the Company's trading

LADY SHAW STEWART *Brigantine*   *181 tons*   *T & J Brocklebank*   *1827*

Remarks:

Also rigged as a Brigantine but with slightly larger overall dimensions than the previous vessels built for Jefferson's.

The majority of the shares in the ownership of the' Lady Shaw Stewart' were held by the Jefferson family (56 out of 64). Captain John Taylor, earlier in command of the 'Thetis' (in 1824), held the remaining eight shares.

However, shortly after purchase of this vessel, the Jefferson's sold their shares to a Mr Wilson Penny, a Whitehaven Merchant. The 'Lady Shaw Stewart' remained registered to the Jefferson's and it can be assumed that the Jefferson's were acting for the new owner in some capacity, probably as Agents or Managing Owners.

This vessel carried out numerous voyages between Whitehaven and Antigua between 1827 and 1846 when it was sold to a Captain Roper. The number of different Masters was also notable in those nineteen years. They included names already mentioned as commanding other vessels in the Jefferson Fleet, such as: Captains John Taylor; Henry Booth Hewitt; Robert McCormick; William Steele; Thomas James and Joseph Wise.

The steady stream of traffic between Whitehaven and Antigua during those years indicates that trade must have been very brisk indeed. Consider also that the Jefferson's were not the only Merchants from Whitehaven and other English Ports, plying their trade between England and the West Indies.

DERWENT	*Brigantine*	*221 tons*	*Jonathan Fell* *Workington*	*1834*

Remarks:

Another Brigantine, again of a larger tonnage and greater overall dimensions.

The 'Derwent' was wholly owned by the Jefferson family. For some reason, between the years 1842 and 1853, ownership switched to other parties at various times; three different owners in total, two of them Masters who had previously commanded Jefferson vessels. Ownership returned to the Jefferson's in 1853 and remained with them until 1863 when the vessel was finally sold to a Captain Moat. There are no Lloyds Registers after 1869.

Voyages completed under the different Masters were:

Whitehaven –Antigua	*1834*	*Captain Wilson Harper*
Whitehaven – Rio	*1834*	*Captain Henry Booth Hall*
Liverpool – Canton		
(China)	*1836*	*-do-*

In August 1836 the command of this vessel passed to a Captain William Steele

Whitehaven – Antigua		
- London	*1838*	*Captain Wilson Harper**
? - Whampoa	*1848*	*Captain William Steele (for Messrs*
		M'Minn (a new owner since 18412
From Antigua	*1853*	*Captain J Bell**
Whitehaven – (		
West Indies (	*1855*	*-do-**
(	*1856*	*-do-**
(	*1857*	*-do-**
Liverpool – (		
West Indies (	*1858*	*-do-**
(	*1859*	*-do-**
(	*1860*	*Captain Moat**
Whitehaven –		
West Indies	*1863*	*Captain Moat (Master and New Owner)*

- *These voyages were on behalf of the Jefferson's*

BRITISH QUEEN *Brigantine* *218 tons* *Lumley Kennedy#* *1838*
Whitehaven

Remarks:

A Brigantine, of similar size to the 'Derwent'.

Wholly owned by the Jefferson's. By then they had been trading for some years as Robert and Henry Jefferson, Wine Merchants, Whitehaven. (Robert (1) and Henry (1))

Voyages made:

Whitehaven – Antigua	*1838*	*Captain*	*Thomas Kennedy*
-do-	*1839*		*-do-*
Whitehaven – Antigua			
- Liverpool	*1840-1845*		
	(five voyages)		*-do-*
-do-	*1846-1852*	*Captain Joseph Wise*	
-do-	*1853*	*Captain Andrew Hunter*	
-do-	*1854-1858*	*Captain Joseph Wise*	
-do-	*1859-1860*	*Captain Joseph Ledger*	
From ? to West Indies			
and Newfoundland	*1861*	*Captain William Hinde*	

Note: The 'British Queen' was lost off the coast of Newfoundland on the 6th May 1861. No records are available at the time of writing to show if there was any loss of life. A small Oil painting of this vessel is on display at 'The Rum Story'

It was possible in those days to complete several voyages between England and the West Indies within a year. Generally, the voyages started and ended at Whitehaven, after berthing at Liverpool.+

The reason why Captain Hunter acted as Master of the 'British Queen' in 1853 was simply because the regular Master, Joseph Wise, was engaged on private family business during that time.

 # Mention of this Firm is made at the end of this Shipping List.

+ As stated earlier Liverpool gradually assumed prominence over Whitehaven as a major English Port.

MIDGE *Sloop* *28 tons* *Lumley Kennedy* *1840*

Remarks:

Wholly owned by the Jefferson's.

This tiny vessel was a 'Sloop' (later termed a 'Smack'). It was only 41 feet (a little over 12 metres) in length. A Sloop is a single-masted, fore-and-aft rigged sailing vessel with only one headsail. In the Eighteenth century, the term 'Sloop' was also used for any small Naval vessel. A 'Smack' is also a single-masted sailing boat used for coasting or fishing. At first, it is difficult to understand why the Jefferson's commissioned such a small vessel. However, this became clear after its first voyage, in 1840/1841, to Cadiz in Spain, Master, Captain Thomas James. The 'Midge' returned to Cadiz in 1841 from Whitehaven and continued on to Antigua under the same Master (incidentally with future Captain Joseph Wise as 'Mate'.) From 1842, the 'Midge' was used by the Jefferson's in Antigua until sold in December 1843 to a George Athil of Antigua..

| ANTIGUA | Barque | 287.7 tons | H & G Barrick | 1858 |
| | | | Whitby | |

Remarks:

The 'Antigua' was a Barque which is a sailing vessel with three or more masts. The aftermost mast is fore-and-aft rigged and the remainder are square-rigged. This style was prevalent in the last decade of the Nineteenth century, as a last stand against the competition from Steam ships, but, ultimately, Sail was forced to give way to Steam.

The 'Antigua' was, to date, the largest vessel owned by the Jefferson family. With The exception of the 'Midge', it was more or less a gradual progress up the scale in tonnage for the Jefferson Fleet.

Although the 'Antigua' was not wholly owned by the Jefferson's, again, the majority of the shares were held by family members. Of a total of sixty-four shares, fifty-six were held by the family and eight by Captain Joseph Wise.

Voyages:

Whitehaven – Antigua	1858	Captain Joseph Wise
Whitehaven – Antigua		
-Trinidad	1859	-do-
Liverpool – Antigua	1860-1862	-do-
-do-	1863-1864	Captain Joseph Morgan
Liverpool – West		
Indies	1865-1868	-do-
Liverpool – Belfast		
- West Indies	1869	Captain John Wood
-do-	1870-1871	Captain Daniel McLean
Liverpool – Hamburg	1872	Captain Francis .T Calf
London – West		
Indies	1873-1880	-do-

Note: The 'Antigua' was sold on the 15th October 1880 to Messrs H.S.van Gauten of Holland.

Captain John Wood was a Cumbrian; Captain Daniel McLean was an Irishman from County Down; Captain Joseph Morgan was Whitehaven-born (in 1824).

EHEN   *Barque*   *301.3*   *Lumley Kennedy*   *1863*

Remarks:

Another Barque, of greater tonnage than the earlier 'Antigua' and of greater overall dimensions.

Again, although not wholly owned by the family, the majority of shares were held by the Jefferson's. Out of sixty-four shares, forty-eight were held by family members. Two non-family shareholders, George Robinson of Carlisle and Captain Joseph Wise each held eight shares. The main shareholding amongst the Jefferson's was that of the two senior members, Henry (2) and Robert (3) of Rothersyke.

Voyages:

Liverpool – Lima –		
Callao (Peru)	*1864*	*Captain Joseph Wise*
Liverpool – Buenos		
Aires – Whitehaven	*1865*	*-do-*
Whitehaven –		
Barbados	*1866*	*-do-*
Liverpool – Antigua)		
Liverpool – Barbados)	*1867*	*-do-*
Liverpool – Antigua		
- Alcoa Bay	*1868*	*-do-*
Liverpool – Barbados		
- Bahia	*1869*	*-do-*
Liverpool – Rio –		
Barbados-	*1870*	*-do-*
Liverpool - ?	*1871*	*-do-*
Liverpool - ?	*1872-1873*	*Captain Albert Henry Hume*
Liverpool - ?	*1874-1877*	*Captain Joseph Morgan*
	1878 (see below)	

1878: Ownership passed to Captain Lewis Evans of Liverpool.
The 'Ehen' was then captained by a relative, Captain David Evans.
After further changes of ownership the 'Ehen' was sold, finally,
in 1888, to a French Shipowner/Master who apparently changed the name
of the vessel after re-registering it in France, at Le Havre.

PATNA   *Barque*   *362 tons*   *T & J Brocklebank*   *1842*

Remarks:

A Barque, the largest vessel, in terms of tonnage, owned by the Jefferson's.

All the shares in the 'Patna' were held by the family on Brocklebank's sale to them after the vessel's completion date.

Voyages:

Whitehaven – West Indies	1869	Captain Joseph Morgan
Whitehaven – Cork –		
West Indies	1870-1872	-do-
Cork-West Indies		
- Liverpool – Mauritius	1877	-do-
(until 1883?)		

Note: The 'Patna' was sold to Messrs W.R. Kelly of Whitehaven and traded in coastal waters under Captain T Evans until broken up in 1886. The Barque had therefore spent an astonishing forty-four years at sea.

It has not been possible to establish the reason(s) for the occasional changeover of Masters of the various vessels in the Jefferson Fleet. It may well be one or more of the following:

The great variety of work available to Merchantmen at that time of increasing prosperity in the country, where there was access to products previous unobtainable except at great expense and thus, perhaps, giving the Master some choice in what cargo he wished to transport and from where he would need to collect it – exotic destinations!

A choice of destinations, not just to the West Indies, but to North and South America and Canada; the Mediterranean, etc. Weather conditions and time of year would probably play an important part in any decisions, bearing in mind the heavy seas in the Atlantic and the tiny and relatively flimsy ships of the time.

Quality of seamanship would also play a major part in any decision by the Shipowner of whom to hire for a particular voyage. There would also be additional inducements such as an offer of bonuses for speedy completion of round trips.

Opportunity to work for different Shipowners, thus gaining experience and becoming 'known' to those in a position to offer employment.

Of the ten ships in the Jefferson Fleet, eight were built in Whitehaven; the first, the 'Gale' in 1758 by ??????; three, the 'Doris, 'Lady Shaw Stewart' and the 'Patna' by Thomas and John Brocklebank; three, the 'Derwent', 'British Queen' and 'Ehen' by Lumley Kennedy; one, the 'Thetis'by William Wilson. The 'Patna'.built im 1842, was

*the last ship built for the Jefferson's. Of the remaining two vessels, one was built at
Workington and the other at Whitby.*

*Unfortunately, many years ago, the Jefferson business records, from the start of the
business in 1785 to 1813, were lost in a disastrous fire. There is no report of this fire
in the local newspaper of the time, The Cumberland Pacquet. Also lost, according to
one of the surviving family members, but not at the same time, were all the family
photographs. Therefore, there is nothing pictorially to connect the individual
members of the family with their exploits in Shipping and Merchanting, apart from
some old photographs or illustrations in ancient copies of the Whitehaven News.
These generally refer to Obituaries. A number of business records have also not
survived, having been damaged by mildew and the ravages of time. The Cumbria
Record Offices at Carlisle and Whitehaven however hold the remaining family
business records. In addition, at 'The Rum Story', a permanent exhibition at
Jefferson's original premises in Lowther Street, Whitehaven, there are many artefacts
on view and a very interesting commentary on the family and also on the history of
Rum and Slavery. The 'The Rum Story' is mentioned elsewhere in this book.*

*The operation of the Company's Vessels was controlled from Liverpool, a Ship
Brokers' Office having been opened in that city by the Jefferson's. Henry (2)
Jefferson (1800-1877) formed a partnership with a Mr Taylor for this purpose.*

*The Ships owned by the Jefferson family usually started and ended all their voyages in
Whitehaven. They all called at Liverpool and London on the outward journey.*

*The Fleet Vessels plied their trade mainly between England and the West Indies,
carrying Sugar, Rum and Molasses. They also imported Sherry and Port from Spain
and Portugal; Olive Oil and Hams from Spain too; Champagne from France and,
surprisingly, 'Superior' Irish Whiskey and 'Limerick' Prime Beef and Pork from
Ireland. Even in those days there must have been many discriminating clients for
these goods, to make the importation viable. Advertising of these products was a
regular feature in the local Press.*

*'Fine Old West India (sic) Madeira' was also advertised by Jefferson's, in 1835,
being part of the cargo from the 'Thetis'.*

*Most of the sugar came from the Jefferson's Estate in Antigua, 'Yeamans'. A
separate Chapter is devoted to this vitally important Antigua side of the Jefferson's
involvement. The well-known and later famous:*

JEFFERSON'S
FINE
OLD RUM

*was imported from the Yeaman's Estate. The Sherry, imported from Spain and
Portugal was reputed to be shipped to the West Indies and back in butts and
hogsheads as it was maintained that the additional sea voyage improved the flavour.
There is no evidence to support this story but it should be given some credence as
there would be little point in shipping 'dead' cargo over a considerable distance*

without some benefit to the Owners, bearing in mind that shipping space was expensive and also, at times, at a premium.

There is an interesting note in the firm's records regarding one voyage made by the 'Thetis'.

'Left Montego Bay, Jamaica, 10 October 1828, arrived Whitehaven 11 December – sixty-two days; distance by log 5,917 miles. Crew: Captain, mate, carpenter, cook, three seamen and two boys. Cargo: rum twenty-two hogsheads, forty-five puncheons, thirty-one tierces; sugar twelve hogsheads, one barrel, eighty-six tierces; limejuice twenty-one hogsheads, four pipes, one puncheon; coffee thirty-five barrels, twenty tierces; pimento sixty-five bags; molasses seven puncheons; ginger ten barrels; fustic fourteen tons; timber sixty-five logs of mahogany, one log of cedar, and twenty-two spars of lancewood'.

Explanation of terms used above:

Butt:	A cask, typically used for wine, ale or water (a liquid measure equal to 126 US gallons – 477.5 litres)
Puncheon:	A large cask holding 72-120 Imperial Gallons
Pipe:	A cask for wine, especially as a measure equal to two hogsheads, equal to 105 Imperial Gallons
Hogshead:	Measure of capacity for wine equal to 52.5 Imperial Gallons
Barrel:	A measure of capacity equal to 36 Imperial Gallons
Tierce:	A measure of wine equal to one-third of a pipe, usually equivalent to 35 Imperial Gallons
Pimento:	Red sweet peppers
Fustic:	A yellow dye obtained from either of two kinds of timber, especially that of Old Fustic* *Old Fustic: a tropical tree with heartwood that yields dyes and other products
Spar:	Thick, strong pole for masts or yardarms on a ship
Lancewood:	Any of a number of hardwood trees with tough elastic Timber. A Caribbean tree (*oxandra lanceolate*)

APPENDIX 'B'

EXTRACT FROM SHIP'S DIARY
THE BRIG '*THETIS*'
(Henry Jefferson)

18th January 1824

Wind stronger today – ship seldom going lefs
sic *(less) than 8 Knots before it. Was very wild all day.*
Had a roast leg of Mutton & Apple Dumpling to dinner.
Saw two sail about 8 am, one of them an English Brig
the other Spanish or Portuguese. Observed today a great
increase in the length of the day having had a good Light
at 6 o' clock pm as they will have in Whitehaven at _ past
4.

19th

Strong breeze & cloudy - ship going 7 to 8 1/2 Knots.
During the last 24 Hours she has run up-wards of 190
miles - yesterday even at 6 pm were going 10 Knots by the
Log – very little change in the climate as yet – the Sun has
not favoured us with a glance these three days –
breakfasted the last three days from Oatmeal Porridge

which I found rather too many (?) for this confinement
& want of exercise you undergo during a sea voyage.
Saw a great many porpoise today – and of them many white
which Capt. Taylor says is of the whale species. It seemed
much larger than its companions & many I had previously
seen   …………………..(Unreadable)………………..
which is very amusing. Have not seen a single sail today
or anything living except the certainty of our own little Ark
– the porpoises excepted.

THE JEFFERSON'S OF WHITEHAVEN

APPENDIX 'C'

EXTRACT FROM SHIP'S DIARY: 1828
(Henry Jefferson)

Brig *Thetis* laying at Montego Bay

Date	Remarks and Transactions on Board 1828
Wednesday August 13th	This day Log commences with fine clear weather. Moored ship secured the Yards and landed the 4 Horses safe. Sent 10 empty Water Casks on Shore. Latter part employed clearing the deck made all ready for discharging Mr Robert Martin after using some very abusive language to the Captain and refusing to Work was sent on shore at his own request. Ends Calm and Clear Weather………………
Thursday August 14th	These 24 hours begin Light variable Winds with heavy Rain. Hoisted the Long Bat out and Landed 3000 Pieces of Red Oak Staves. Carpenter caulking the Bright Work outside Shipped Adam Smartt the Hostler as Seaman. Ends Calm and Cloudy Weather……………
Friday August 15th	These 24 hours begin steady Breezes and Cloudy Weather. People employed discharging – Landed 7528 Red Oak Staves 1 Bar =rel of Flour and 800 Pieces of White Oak Heading Latter Part Variable Winds and heavy Rain. Carpenter caulking the Paint Work outside. 2 Men and two Brats hired from Shore. Ends Calm and Cloudy Weather.
Saturday August 16th	This days Log begins Cloudy and Light Winds. Landed 1097 Pieces of White Oak Heading and 4990 Pieces of Red Oak Staves. Latter Part D ? Weather unbent all the Sails. Ends Light Winds and Clear Weather. 2 Men and two Brats …..? Carpenter as above.
Sunday August 17th	These 24 hours throughout steady Breezes and Cloudy Weather. Received on Board fresh Beef for all hands.
Monday	This day People employed discharging Landed 50 Barrels of

August 18th Indian Corn Meal, 64 Barrels of flour, 700 pieces of White Oak Heading and 4200 Red Oak Staves. Got the Derrick up 2 Men and two Brats hired. Carpenter caulking the Ship outside. Weather as Yesterday.

Dates	Remarks and Transactions on Board 1828	Dates
Wednesday August 13th Received on Board Beef for all Hands.	This days log commences with fine clear Weather. Moored Ship & secured the Yards and Landed the 4 Horses safe. — Sent 10 empty Water Casks on Shore. Latter part employed cleaning the decks made all ready for discharging & c Robert Martin after using some very abusive Language to the Captain and refusing to Work was sent on shore at his own request — Ends Calm and Clear Weather. —	Tuesday August 1st Wednes-day August
Thursday August 14th	These 24 hours begin light Variable Winds with heavy Rain Hoisted the Long Boat out and Landed 3000 Pieces of Red Oak Staves. Carpenter Caulking the Bright Work outside Shipped Adam Smart the hostler as Seaman. — Ends Calm and Cloudy Weather. — — — —	Thursd—a August
Friday August 15th	These 24 hours begin steady Breezes and Cloudy Weather. — People employed discharging Landed 7538 Red Oak Staves 1 Barrel of Flour and 800 Pieces of White Oak Heading. Latter Part Variable Winds and heavy Rain. Carpenter Caulking the Paint Work outside. 2 Men and two Boats hired from shore Ends Calm and Cloudy Weather. — — — —	Friday August —
Saturday August 16th	This days log begins Cloudy and light Winds. — Landed 1097 Pieces of White Oak Heading and 4990 Pieces of Red Oak Staves Latter part Dirty Weather unbent all the Sails. Ends light Winds and Clear Weather 2 Men and two Boats hired Carpenter as above. — — —	Satur—a Augu— Broa— the 5th or Bread.
Sunday August 17th	These 24 hours throughout steady Breezes and Cloudy Weather. Received on Board fresh Beef for all Hands. —	Sund— Augu—
Monday August 18th	This day People employed discharging Landed 50 Barrels of Indian Corn Meal, 64 Barrels of Flour, 900 Pieces of White Oak Heading and 4200 Red Oak Staves. Got the Derrick up 2 Men and two Boats hired. Carpenter Caulking the Ship outside Weather as Yesterday. —	

APPENDIX 'D'

EXTRACT FROM SHIP'S LOG: 1828
(Henry Jefferson)

Brig *Thetis* from Jamaica towards Whitehaven

H	K	F	Courses	Winds	LW	Remarks on Board Monday November 10th
2	1		North	E N E		This day Log Commenced with Light
4						Air inclining to Calm
6			Calm Shiphead			
8			round the ??			
10						
12						At midnight Calm and Cloudy
2						
4						
6	1		E by N/ N	??		At 4 A M a Light Air from the S.
8	1	4				
10	2	4				At 10 A M set the Starboard Steering
12	2					Sails.
-------						People employed repairing sails etc.
16	Miles distance Per Log					At noon Light Winds and Cloudy
						with Small Rain

Sun obscure

H	K	F	Courses	Winds	LW	Remarks on Board Tuesday November 11th
2	2		E	N by S		This Day's Log Commences Light Winds and
				N W		Cloudy Weather.
4	2					
6	2	4				
8	2	4		North		Bent all the Sails afresh and unbent the
						square mainsail to repair and Bent an
10	3	4				another one.
12	4					At 4 P M Shifted the Lower and fore top
2	4					mast steering sail to the Larboard Side

```
 4  4                          At 7 P M took in the Starboard M Top
 6  2 4  E by S   N              Steering Sail
 8  2     E S E   -----
10 2    S S E/ .E  East         At midnight a Steady Breeze and
                                  and Cloudy Weather
12 1 4  S E     E N E           At 10 A M in all Steering Sails
   -------                       People employed repairing Sails
   66     Miles distance per Log At noon Light Winds inclining to
                                  Calm and Cloudy Weather
```

                         de   d   o
                 Lat   Obs   30.5 North

Brig Thetis from Jamaica towards Whitehaven

H	K	F	Courses	Winds	w	Remarks on Board Monday November 11th
2	1		North	E.N.E		This days log commences with light
4						airs inclining to Calm. —
6						
8			Calm	Ships head		
10			round the Compass			At midnight Calm and Cloudy
12						
2						
4						At 4 o'clk a light air from the
6	1		E by N p.m	N.W.bN		
8	1	4				At 10 A.M set the Starboard Steering
10	2	4				
12	2					Sails employed repairing Sails &c
	16		Miles distance Per Log			People employed repairing Sails &c
						At noon light N airs and Cloudy
						with Small Rain. —
						⊙ Sun Obscure. —

H	K	F	Courses	Winds	w	Remarks on Board Tuesday Novr 11th
2	2		E t —	N.b.S		This Days log commences light N airs and
4	2			N.W.b½		Cloudy Weather. —
6	2	4				Bent all the Sails afresh and unbent the
8	2	4	———	North		Spare main sail to repair and Bent an
10	3	4				other one —
12	4					At 4 P.M shifted the lower and fore top
2	4					mast Steering sail to the larboard side
4	4					At 7 P.M took in the Starboard N top
6	2	4	E by S	N.E.b.E½		Steering Sail —
8	2		E S E			At midnight a Steady Breeze and
10	2		S S E b E	E.b.S		Cloudy Weather —
12	1	4	S E	E.N.E		At 10 A.M in all Steering Sails —
	66		Miles distance Per Log			People employed repairing Sails &c
						At noon Light Winds inclining to
						Calm and Cloudy Weather —
						Lat de ⊙ Obr ½ 50.5′ North

155

APPENDIX 'E'

EXTRACT FROM SHIP'S LOG: 1828
(Henry Jefferson)

Brig *Thetis* from Jamaica towards Quebec

H K F Courses Winds LW   Remarks on Board Wednesday May 14th

H K F	Courses	Winds	Remarks
2 2 4	N E	E S E	These 24 hours begin steady Breeze and clear Weather.
4 3 4	N E by N		
6 4 4	N by W	N E by E	
8 3 4	N N E	East	Got the anchor? on the sails and bent the
10 3			Hemp Cable.
12 1 4			
1 4	S E by E		
2 2 4	S E		At 10 P M took in the staysails flying jibs
4 4			
6 3	S E by E/2 E		At midnight Light Winds and hazy Weather
8 3	South E		
10 2			
2	North		At 9 A M tacked to the North set Staysails flying jib etc.
12 5 4	North		

------

75 Miles distance Per Log

------   At Noon steady Breezes and hazy Weather

de   d   o
Lat   Obs   45.22'N not to be
depended on very hazy.

H K F Courses Winds LW Remarks on Board Thurdsay May 15th

H K F	Courses	Winds	Remarks
2 5	N by W	N E by E	These 24 hours begin steady Breezes and
4 4			thick foggy Weather

```
6  4  4   S E by S    E by N
8  3  4   S E by E ?  East          At 4 P M Cape Portland.  Bore N N E 1 Mile?
10 4  4                             tacked to the S East
12 4  4   S by E
2  4      S by E                    At 11 P M took in the flying Jib.
4  3
6  4      N E        E S E          At midnight steady Breezes and cloudy Weather
8  3  4   N E/2 E                    took in the staysails.
10 5  4   N E by N                  At 4 A M  tacked to the N E set Staysails
12 5                                At 10 A M set flying jib
-----
102 Miles Distance Per Log
-----
```

At noon steady Breezes and thick
Foggy Weather set the Starboard fore
Top mast steering sail.

          de   *d*   *o*
Lat   Obs   45 35' North

Brig Thetis from Jamaica towards Quebec

H	K	F	Courses	Winds	
2	2	4	N E	E S E	Remarks on Board Wednesday May 14th 1828
4	5	4	N E ½ N		These 24 hours begin steady Breezes and clear
6	4	4	N ½ N	N E ½ E	Weather
8	3	4	N N E	East	Got the anchors on the rails and bent the
10	3				Hemp Cable
12	1	4	S E ½ E		At 10 P M took in the topsails flying Jib &c
2	2	4	S E	E N E	At 11 P M tack'd to the S E
4	2	4	S E ½ S		At midnight light Winds and hazy Weather
6	3		S E ½ E ½ E		At 9 P M tacked to the N and set Staysails
8	3		S E ½ E		flying Jib &c
11	2		North		
12	5	4	N 72 W		At noon steady Breezes and hazy Weather
	77		Miles distance Per log		
					Latd. Obsd. 45..45 &c Nd not to be
					depended on very hazy

H	K	F	Courses	Winds	
2	5		N ½ N	N E ½ E	Remarks on Board Thursday May 15th
4	4	4	S E ½ S	E ½ N	These 24 hours begin steady Breezes and
6	3	4	S ½ E ½ E	East	thick foggy Weather
4	4	4	S E E		At 4 P M Cape Portland Bore N N E 5 Miles
12	4	4	S ½ E		tacked to the S East
2	4		S ½ E		At 11 P M took in the flying Jib
4	3				At midnight steady Breezes and cloudy Weather
6	4		N E	E S E	took in the staysails
8	5	4	N E ½ E		At 4 A M tacked to the N E set Staysail
11	5	4	N E ½ N		At 10 A M set flying Jib
10	5				At noon steady Breezes and thick
	102		Miles Distance Per log		foggy Weather set the Starboard fore
					top mast steering Sail
					Latd. Obsd. 45..55 North

158

THE JEFFERSON'S OF
WHITEHAVEN

APPENDIX 'F'

SHORT EXTRACT FROM SHIP'S LOG
THE BRIG *'THETIS'*
(HENRY JEFFERSON)

11th January 1824

*Sailed from Whitehaven in the Brig Thetis, Capt
John Taylor, bound for Antigua, at _ past 6
o' clock AM.   Wind S.E.*

*7PM. Day remarkably fine and clear wind
varying from SE to W. Kept perfectly fine from
sickness all day. Read a couple of cantos of
Don Juan and two or three newspapers. Saw
Very few sails this day. Towards 9PM began
To blow rather fresh, had an uncomfortable
night.*

Author's Note:

More detail on Henry (2) Jefferson's voyages to
and from the West Indies c an be found in
Appendix 'D' of 'From Cumberland to Cape
Horn'. By D.Hollett (see Acknowledgments/

Bibliography to this book)

Deeds and related papers regarding Plantations
in Antigua, including Conveyance, including list
Of 400 slaves of a plantation formerly owned by
Ogilvy were withdrawn by Whitehaven
Development Co.

THE JEFFERSON'S OF
WHITEHAVEN

APPENDIX 'G'

Extracts from Personal Diary of Robert Henry Jefferson;
1844 (February; March; April; May; June; August)
(Mansfield Commercial Diary for 1844)

4 SUNDAY [35]   Septuagesima Sunday. Full Moon,
    8. 43 morn.

5 MONDAY [36]   *Agatha.*

8 THURSDAY [39]

6 TUESDAY [37]

British Queen sailed for Antigua

9 FRIDAY [40]

7 WEDNESDAY [38]

10 SATURDAY [41]   Queen Victoria married.

---

24 SUNDAY [84]   5 Sunday in Lent.

25 MONDAY [85]   Annunciation. Lady Day.

Advise Bills due April 14th 1844
1351 Wm Brown due Do Lo £100
No 1352 Antigua Rect f. drawn by A. Auchinleck
in favour of Paul Horsford 90ds ½ £100
No 1353 Antigua Rect f. A. Auchinleck Lucas of Engr
in favour of A. Crawford 90ds ⅔ £150. .0

28 THURSDAY [88]

advised March 28h
Do Do
Do Do

26 TUESDAY [86]   Prince George of Cambridge b.

Insurance p Lady Shaw Stewart –
Ship & Cargo.
query fully covered. –

29 FRIDAY [89]   Cambridge Term ends.

ordered £ 5 000 March 28h

27 WEDNESDAY [87]   Moon, First Quar. 5. 2. morn.

30 SATURDAY [90]   Oxford Term ends.

Rect. Child &c Per Martin's
balance my account

31 SUNDAY [91] Palm Sunday.

1 APRIL. MONDAY [92]

4 THURSDAY [95] *Maundy Thursday. St. Ambrose.*

Advice Bill due April 24th 1844

No 1355 Antigua Bill 93rd 1844 drawn by Will. Byam Esq? of the of Clithoro's Estate in favour of W. Simpson Lent. 90 at 7% £100

advice April

2 TUESDAY [93]

5 FRIDAY [96] Good Friday.

3 WEDNESDAY [94] *Rich. Bp. Chich.* Full Moon,
   6. 58. morning.

6 SATURDAY [97] *Old Lady Day.*

---

28 SUNDAY [119] 3 Sunday after Easter.

29 MONDAY [120]

2 THURSDAY [123] Full Moon, 3. 16. aftern.

Kyanite sailed from Antigua

30 TUESDAY [121]

3 FRIDAY [124] *Invention of the Cross.*

1 MAY. WEDNESDAY [122] *St. Philip and James.*

4 SATURDAY [125]

23 SUNDAY [175] 3 Sunday after Trinity. Moon,
First Quar. 3. 24. aftern.

24 MONDAY [176] Nat. John Bapt. *Mids. Day.*

Advise Bill due 1 July/44

1365 Antigua March 12th.

S Auchenleck Yeamans Trust Estate
for £120
*   Advised this day —*

25 TUESDAY [177]

26 WEDNESDAY [178]

27 THURSDAY [179]

Advise Bill due July 15/44

1366 Antigua 5 March 1844,

C F Lipscombe   £100 —
*   — Advised — July 1/44 —*

28 FRIDAY [180] Qu. Victoria crowned.

29 SATURDAY [181] St. Peter.

---

18 SUNDAY [231] 11 Sunday after Trinity.

19 MONDAY [232]

20 TUESDAY [233]

Advise Bills

1377   S Auchenleck   £215.11
1378   Henry Jefferson   120 —
1379   S Auchenleck   200 —
*   £535.11*

Advised 22

21 WEDNESDAY [234] Moon, First Quar. 2. 16. morn.

22 THURSDAY [235]

23 FRIDAY [236]

24 SATURDAY [237] St. Bartholomew.

Advise Bill

1380   C F Lipscomb   225

Advised
Aug 2/44

APPENDIX 'H'

Extract from Merchants' Directory (c 18th century?)
Personal copy of Henry Jefferson.
Signed on flyleaf 'Henry Jefferson'
(Pages 165-170 relate to Whitehaven)

r the Hand of the Clerk, is to be fixed upon the utside of the Door of the *Moothall*, or on the Mar-t Place of the Town of *Colchester*.

Persons accepting of any Place of Profit, or other rust relative to the said Duties, or farming any Kay ithin the Limits of this Act, are made incapable of ting as Commissioners.

The Prescriptive, or other Rights of the Borough *Colchester*, are to continue and remain the same, if this Act had not been made, in all Things not terfering with the Directions and due Execution ereof.

All Suits or Actions, to be brought for any thing done nder any of the former Acts, shall be commenced ithin six Months after the Commencement of this ct; and if any Action or Suit shall be brought for ny Thing that shall be done in Pursuance of any of ie said former Acts, or this present Act, shall be ommenced in six Months after the Fact committed, nd shall be brought in the County of *Essex*; and ie Defendants may plead the General

ssue, that the same was done by the   p. 589. uthority of the former Acts, or this

ct; and if it so appear, or if the Suit be brought n any other County, the Jury shall find for the De-endants; or if the Plaintiffs become Nonsuit, or iscontinue their Action, or a Verdict pass against hem, or on Demurrer Judgment is given against hem, the Defendants shall have treble Costs, on the Certificate of the Judge before whom the Cause was ried, and shall have the same Remedy as Defendants ave for Costs in other Cases by Law.

This Act shall be deemed a public Act, and shall e judicially taken Notice of as such by all Judges, &c. without specially pleading the same.

WHITEHAVEN.

Whereas the Town of *Whitehaven* 7 Ann.n. in the County of *Cumberland*, is of late

Years greatly improved in Trade and Shipping, and is yet capable of farther Improvements therein, to the great Advancement of her Majesty's Revenue, the Increase of Shipping and Navigation, and the Benefit of the said Inhabitants, and of the adjacent Country, if the Harbour of the said Town can be preserved, in the Harbour of the said Town can be preserved, in a proper Manner: And whereas the Application of the accustomed Du-ties, besides several very considerable Sums, are found insufficient to defray the growing Charges of maintaining the said Harbour, and of making such new Works as are still necessary for securing it: To the End therefore that such Course may be for ever

---

ever established as shall be effectual for the Purposes aforesaid,

S. 1.   It is enacted, That all that Precinct included within the Limits and Bounds herein after expressed, viz. beginning at the Wharf, on the North-west End of *Marlborough* Street, and from thence in a Line North-east and by North till the Middle of *Lowther* Street, open upon it, and from thence in a streight Line parallel to the *Range* of the same Street, directly to the Low-Wa-ter Mark, from thence, by the Low-Water Mark to the Rock whereon the new Mole is begun to be erect-ed, and so along the said Rocks, by the Low-Water Mark, till it answer the Line of the said Mole, from thence along that Line till it come up to the said Mole, and so along the same Mole, and from thence in-cluding the said Platform, along the new Wharf, till it meet with the Wharf of the West Strand, near the House of *Mary Addison*, Widow, from thence along the said Wharf by the Customhouse Kay, in a streight Line to the West Side of the Timber-Yard, and so along the Wall of the said Yard, to the North-west Corner thereof, and from thence by the North-west Wall of the same Yard to the Wharf where it began, as the same has lately been set out and bounded, is, and shall be from henceforth for ever, the Harbour of *Whitehaven* aforesaid, and ap-propriated to the lying, anchoring, and mooring of all such Ships, Vessels, and Boats, as shall have Oc-casion at any Time or Times hereafter to make Use of the same, and to no other Purpose whatsoever.

S. 2.   No Houses, Enclosures, or Build-ings whatsoever, shall at any Time hereafter be made nearer the said Harbour, than is hereafter limited, viz. On the West Strand nearer than the present Houses, &c. there, on the new Wharf between Mrs. *Walker's* House, and the North-east Corner of *Henry Walker's* Ground-plot, nearer than the Range of the said House and Ground, and from thence to the Iron Oar Steaths, nearer than forty-eight Yards at *Henry Wal-ker's*, drawn to forty Yards, at the said Steaths; from thence to the North-east Corner of the same, Steaths, nearer than the East Range of the same, eighteen Yards; and from thence to the Platform, nearer than the Range of *Howsen's* Smithy, and from the Platform along the new Mole, to the El-bow of the said Mole, nearer than twelve Yards, and from thence to the Low-water Mark, nearer than a Line stretching to the North-west, and along the Counter Mole intended to be made on the

North-east Side of the said the Range of the North-east nor from thence to the Tin fifteen Yards; but that all be left free and open for t the Mooring of Ships and V of common Wharfs or Kay the Shipping in Repairs or thing shall be taken or dem Account of Wharfage, for t Wharfs or Kays, nor for *James Lowther*, Esq; or hi or more of the Trustees he agree to erect or make any t Engine, on the said Wharfs they are hereby impowered convenient, for the better any Goods, in which Case Recompence shall be paid Harbour, by such Mercha willing to make use of the f

Provided, that the said ther, his Heirs, &c. Lords nor of *St. Bees*, in the said *Cumberland*, shall and may tinue the Watch-house, an and the Store Room at th pair and rebuild the same, Profits thereof to his and t

A sufficient Way, open Carts, and other Carriag left along each of the fai said Pier, and through t *Walker's* Ground Plot and the Ground of the said same Wharf, not less th joining upon the said Ste contained to the contrar

And as it is found nece plete and finish the new said, and to make a Coun Head on the North-east S strengthen and repair the and other Works, and to Harbour; be it farther e aforesaid accustomed Du have been heretofore us are hereby wholly and s charged; there shall be p of *March*, 1709, for al then next ensuing, th herein after mentioned, ry Ton, computing 1

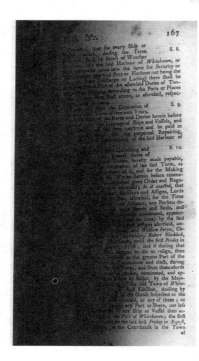

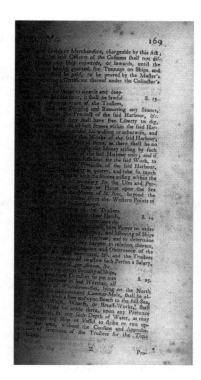

... Goods or Merchandize, chargeable by this Act; ... and Officers of the Customs shall not dis-... any Ship outwards, or inwards, until the ... hereby granted, for Tonnage on Ships and ... shall be paid, to be proved by the Master's ... Certificate thereof under the Collector's ...

the better to cleanse and deep-... of the said Harbour, it shall be lawful ... or more of the Trustees, ... digging and Removing any Stones, ... the Precinct of the said Harbour, &c. ... they shall have free Liberty to dig, ... all such Stones within the said Har-... for walling or otherwise, and ... the Works of the said Harbour, ... them, as there shall be no ... the Money arising by such ... the said Harbour only; and if ... sufficient for the said Work, to ... Precincts of the said Harbour, ... Liberty to quarry, and take so much ... the Stones arising within the ... necessary for the Uses and Pur-... Place or Places upon the Sea ... Bay of St. Bees, beyond the ... distance from the Western Points of ...

... Trustees ... their Hands, ...

S. 24. ... shall have Power to order ... and Mooring of Ships ... Harbour, and to determine ... happen in relation thereto, ... and Observance of the ... appointed, &c. and the Trustees ... impowered to allow such Person a Salary, ... per Annum, &c.

S. 25. ... for the Security of Ships, ... that cannot be put into ... Approach in bad Weather, all ... Bay, lying on the North ... the intended Counter-Mole, shall be al-... and open Beach to the full Sea, ... Wall, Wharf, &c. Breast-Works, shall ... Time be made there, upon any Pretence ... in any such Depth of Water, as may ... any Ship or Vessel to strike or run up-... the same, without the Consent and Approba-... of Seventeen of the Trustees for the Time ...

Z   Pro-

S. 25. Provided nevertheless, that as the Land shall happen to gain on the Sea, on the North-East Side, of the said Counter-Mole; it shall be lawful, for such Persons, as shall be Owners of such Lands, to advance any Buildings, or other Works, at their Will or Pleasure, so as not to endanger the Striking of any Ship, or Vessel thereon; any Thing herein contained to the contrary thereof notwithstanding.

And as the temporary Duties, granted by this Act, cannot of a long Time
S. 27. raise such a Sum of Money, as may be sufficient for the aforesaid extraordinary Works which are to be done at the said Harbour; It is therefore further enacted, that eleven or more of the said Trustees are hereby impowered by Deed, or Deeds indented under their Hands and Seals, to convey and assure all the said Duties hereby granted, or any Part of them, for all, or any Part of the said Term of fourteen Years, as they shall judge requisite, to any Person or Persons, who shall be willing to lend, or advance, any Sum or Sums of Money thereupon, at Interest, not exceeding the Rate of Six Pounds per Centum per Annum, which Money so lent, or advanced, shall be employed for, and towards the Uses of the said Harbour, according to the true Intent and Meaning of this Act, &c.

S. 28. If any Action, Suit, &c. shall be commenced, &c. against any Person, for any Thing that he shall do in Pursuance of this Act, &c. he may plead the general Issue, &c. And this Act shall be taken, and allowed, in all Courts, as a public Act, &c.

Continued by 10 Annæ for 14 Years.
13 Geo. II. The Preamble recites the Acts 7 and 10 Annæ, and shews their Deficiency; and then this Act continues
p. 311. the said two recited Acts for twenty-
p. 312. one Years, to commence after the 10th
p. 313. Day of April, 1740, except so far as
p. 314. either of them are by this Act enlarged, altered, or otherwise explained.

It is further enacted, that the Trustees appointed by the former, or this present Act, have Power to mortgage all or any Part of the Duties (subject to the forementioned Debt of 938l. 17s. 7¼d.) to any Persons who shall advance Money thereon, to effect the necessary Purposes of this Act, and secure the Repayment of the Sums so advanced, with Interest for the same.

p. 315. The Money directed to be borrowed by this Act, shall be applied in the first Place to discharge the said Sum of

938l. 17s. 7¼d. borrowed by Authority of [the] Acts, with the Interest, and afterwards for such such new Works, as may be necessary for [keeping] the said Harbour, and keeping the same in [re]pair.

After the said Sums are paid off, and the [In]terest judged by the Justices of the Quarter-Sessions, in good Repair, the Temporary Duties [shall be] a Moiety only of the Duties on Tonnage of [Ships] granted by the former Acts, shall continue, [until] the Harbour in repair for ever.

This Act shall be deemed a public Act, &c.
The Rest of the preceding Act is only relat[ing to clean]ing the Roads, and setting up Turnpikes in the [neigh]bourhood of Whitehaven, and consequently ha[s no] Affinity with the Maritime Affairs we are now [treating] of, its Insertion here would be superfluous and [unne]cessary.

GREENOCK.

The Town of Greenock, in the 24 Geo. [II.] County of Renfrew, being advanta- p. 943. geously situated on the River Clyde, for carrying on both foreign and coasting Trade, Superior, with the Inhabitants thereof about [the] Year 1705, began to raise Money by a [volun]Subscription, for building a Harbour there, [and the] Progress hath been made therein, which if com[pleted] would be of great Advantage to the Town, [and to] the Trade and Navigation of those Parts; [but the] Produce of the Subscription has been found [insuffi]cient to answer that Purpose, and to [the Expence] defray the Expence of Cleaning the Harbour, and of performing other Works, which are absolutely necessary [to make] the same useful and commodious: And as the [build]ing of a new Church, Townhouse, &c. are [neces]sary and much wanted, but the Inhabitants [are not] able to raise Money to answer the Expence [and are] nor to complete the Harbour, and keep all [these] Works in Repair, without the Aid of Parlia[ment]: It is enacted, that from and after June 1, 17[?] the Term of thirty-one Years, and to the [end of] the then next Session of Parliament, a Duty [of two] Pennies Scots, or one Sixth Part of a Penny [Sterling] (over and above the Duty of Excise payable [to his] Majesty) shall be laid upon every Scots Pint [of Ale] or Beer, brewed, brought in, tapped, or [sold] in the Town of Greenock, and Baronies of [Easter and] Wester-Greenock, and Finnart, or the [Liberties] thereof; to be paid by the Brewers for Sale, [and Ven]ders thereof, to John Alexander, Writer, ...

THE JEFFERSON'S OF
WHITEHAVEN

APPENDIX 'I'

Extract from:

Cumberland Pacquet

Tuesday February 1ˢᵗ 1825

Henry Jefferson & Sons Advertisement:

ON SALE

AND DAILY EXPECTED TO ARRIVE
10 PUNCHEONS OF VERY SUPERIOR
LIMERICK WHISKY
80 BARRELS LIMERICK PRIME MESS BEEF
6 BARRELS   Do   Do   PORK

APPRENTICES WANTED.

WANTED immediately, One or Two Youths of respectable Connexions, as APPRENTICES to the LINEN and WOOLLEN DRAPERY BUSINESS.—Apply to

CHRISTOPHER WILLIAMSON,
75, Market Place, Whitehaven.

N.B. Through this Medium C. W. returns his sincere Thanks to his Friends and the Public in general, for past Favours, and begs to assure them it shall be his earnest Endeavour at all Times to merit in Future a Continuance of that Patronage and Support hitherto so liberally experienced.—His Stock of Goods is of choice Selection, and consists of stout Blue Broad Cloths from 5s. 6d. to 9s.; and a great Variety of Shades of Colour in Black and Blue Superfines, from 14s. to 28s. per Yard;—and every other Article in the Linen and Woollen Drapery Line, on the most reasonable Terms.

The WATER-PROOF LONDON SILK HAT, so much in repute, and brought to such great Perfection, he is enabled to offer at a much reduced Price, having a regular Monthly Supply from London.—HOSIERY in great Variety—and UMBRELLAS a very large Assortment, from 4s. 6d. upwards.

TEN THOUSAND POUNDS.

READY to Advance on Mortgage of real Estate, and ample value, the sum of TEN THOUSAND POUNDS, at £3 15s. per Cent.

Apply to Messrs. ADAMSON and SON, Solicitors, Whitehaven.

31st January, 1825.

ON SALE,

AND DAILY EXPECTED TO ARRIVE,
10 PUNCHEONS OF VERY SUPERIOR
LIMERICK WHISKEY.
30 BARRELS LIMERICK PRIME MESS BEEF.
6 BARRELS Do. Do. PORK.

HENRY JEFFERSON AND SONS.

January 22, 1825.

ON SALE,

MEMEL RED PINE TIMBER;
AMERICAN YELLOW PINE TIMBER;
QUEBEC WHITE OAK TIMBER;
QUEBEC WHITE OAK PIPE and PUNCHEON STAVES and HEADINGS;
MEMEL RED PINE DEALS, SPARS, and LATHWOOD;
AMERICAN DEALS, SPARS, & LATHWOOD;
PORT WINE, in Bond, of the most choice Quality and favourite Vintages;
COGNAC BRANDY, in Pieces and Hhds.;
HOLLAND'S GENEVA, in ditto.;

AT a Meeting
Whitehaven
in the Chair,

1. It was Re
Meeting that it
Advantage of a M
that one of the C
holden at Whiteh

2. That it Con
the Ward above
Inn, in this Tow
Day of February
noon, for the pu
be deemed prope
of the Quarter S
that Public Noth

3. That these
Lord Lieutenan
Cumberland Pac

Resolved, that
the Chairman fo

24th January,

FOR MO

T
F
to the Captain,
Jan. 6, 1825.

FOR GI

Will sail from
Passage (having
Master on boar
Whitehaven,

TO BE S
Bidder, at
Innkeeper, Low
the 10th Day of

O

THE JEFFERSON'S OF
WHITEHAVEN

APPENDIX 'J'

Extract from the:

Cumberland Pacquet

Tuesday February 1st 1825

Jefferson's Advertisement 'Freight or Passage'
From WHITEHAVEN to ANTIGUA, sailing on or
about 10th February 1825.

Vessel: The fast-sailing Copper ('bottomed') Brig THETIS.

Master: John Taylor

CUMBERLA

And Ware's Whiteha[

"WHERE MODERATION DWELLS, THE SOUL ADMITS DISTINCT IDEAS AND MATUR'D DEBATE; AN EYE IMPA

TUESDAY, FEBRU.

FOR MONTEGO BAY, FALMOUTH, AND PLACES ADJACENT,

THE VOLUNTEER,

Capt. LINDER,

TO sail the first fair wind after the 20th of February. For Freight or Passage apply to the Captain, or

Jan. 6, 1825. THOS. and M. HARTLEY.

FOR ANTIGUA DIRECT.

The fast-sailing coppered Brig THETIS

JOHN TAYLOR, Master,

A CONSTANT TRADER,

Will sail from hence about the 10th of February. For Freight or Passage, apply to

H. AND R. JEFFERSON.

Whitehaven, Jan. 22, 1825.

ON SALE,

MEMEL RED PINE TIMBER;

AMERICAN YELLOW PINE TIMBER;

QUEBEC WHITE OAK TIMBER;

QUEBEC WHITE OAK PIPE and PUNCHEON STAVES and HEADINGS;

MEMEL RED PINE DEALS, SPARS, and LATHWOOD;

AMERICAN DEALS, SPARS, & LATHWOOD;

PORT WINE, in Bond, of the most choice Quality and favourite Vintages;

COGNAC BRANDY, in Pieces and Hhds.;

HOLLAND'S GENEVA, in ditto.;

JAMAICA RUM, in Puncheons, Hhds. and 45 Gallon Casks;—bonded under the latest Excise Regulations.

WINES, FOREIGN and BRITISH SPIRITS of

THE GRAVEL AND STONE, L

HICKMAN'S PILLS are allowe successful Preparation for effectu preventing the future recurrence of thos arise from an imperfect action of the GRAVEL AND STONE, LUMBAGO, PAINS LOINS, SUPPRESSION OF URINE, &c. most innocent ingredients, this truly relieves the suffering patient from th tures of those diseases, without any v the constitution, and requires no confi of diet during its use. It is one of Medicines extant; and its peculiar v have uniformly maintained the highest Sold in Boxes, at 2s. 9d. and 11s. b 4, Cheapside, St. Paul's, London; a Medicine Venders throughout the Un whom may be had PARSON'S HO MEDICINE, an effectual and saf dangerous complaint. In Packets at

R. GIBSON,

PRINTER OF THIS

RESPECTFULLY informs the i town and places adjacent, that fresh supply of Dr. Solomon's Medicin BALM OF GILEAD and the ANT The Cordial is universally resorted nary superiority in all Complaints o laxations of the Solids, Nervous We ious effects of hot climates, and parti quences of intemperance: And the powerful alterative, purifier, and sw and may be confidently relied on as remedy for the Scurvy, Scrofula, K Eruptions, Leprosy, and disorders a

APPENDIX 'K'

Extract from the:

Cumberland Pacquet

1st September 1835

Jefferson's Advertisements : 'On Sale'
Cargo from Antigua.

Vessel: **LOUISA,** *with Sugar and Molasses*
(A Chartered Ship)

Vessel: **THETIS,** *with Sugar, Molasses, Rum*
and 'Fine Old 'WEST INDIA MADEIRA (3 Pipes
and 2 Hogsheads)

Apply to ROBT. & HY. JEFFERSON.

ON SALE,

THE CARGO of the LOUISA, from AN-
TIGUA, consisting of

4 Hhds.
41 Tierces } SUGAR; and
92 Barrels

10 Puncheons of MOLASSES.

Apply to ROBT & HY. JEFFERSON.

On Sale,

THE CARGO of the THETIS, Capt. HARPER,
from ANTIGUA, consisting of

7 Hhds.
18 Tierces } SUGAR;

307 Puncheons,
36 Hhds., } MOLASSES;
11 Barrels,

9 Puncheons,
12 Hhds., } RUM;

3 Pipes, } Fine old WEST INDIA
2 Hhds., } MADEIRA.

ROBT and HY. JEFFERSON.

Lowther Street, August 25th, 1835.

ROBINSON'S BANKRUPTCY.

THE Commissioners in a Fiat in Bankruptcy bearing date the 20th of December, 1834, awarded
and issued forth against JOHN ROBINSON, of
Whitehaven, in the County of Cumberland, Book-
seller, Dealer, and Chapman, intend to meet on the
8th Day of September next, at Eleven o'Clock in the
Forenoon, at the Black Lion Inn, in Whitehaven, in
the said County, to further Audit the Accounts of the
Assignees of the Estate and Effects of the said Bankrupt, under the said Fiat, pursuant to an Act of Parliament made and passed in the Sixth Year of the
Reign of His late Majesty, King George the Fourth,
intituled "An Act to amend the Laws relating to
Bankrupts"; and the said Commissioners also intend
to meet on the same Day, at Twelve of the Clock, at
Noon, and at the same Place, in order to make a
DIVIDEND of the Estate and Effects of the said
Bankrupt, when and where the Creditors who have
not already proved their Debts are to come prepared
to prove the same, or they will be excluded the Benefit
of the said Dividend. And all Claims not then proved
will be disallowed.

M. WALKER, Solicitor.

MILBECK-HALL-FARM, NEAR KESWICK,

APPENDIX 'L'

Extracts from A History of the Churches of the
Rural Deanery of Whitehaven

THE HOLY TRINITY CHURCH

1) *Page 63: Death of Thomas Jefferson; buried in Holy*
    Trinity Churchyard and not St Nicholas's Churchyard as
    claimed in other local histories.

    The 'three other children lying near him' are probably
    John, Daniel and Mary , all children of Robert (1) who
    died in infancy.

2) *Page 64: Death of Robert (1); Martha his widow and*
    Robert (who died in New York and was not directly
    involved in the family's business, therefore not
    'numbered' as are the other 'Roberts' and 'Henrys'.
    Also, Mary.

3) *Page 65: Marriage of Robert (1) Jefferson and Martha*
    Skelton and a brief obituary to Robert (1).

4) *Page 71: Deaths of Henry (1) and Robert (2) Jefferson.*
    Other lesser family members are also mentioned on

5.—Silver Paten, 9½ inches in diameter.
Inscribed :—

"1773
Trinity Chapel
Messrs. Rd. Bowman and Jo. Burrow,
Junior, Chapel Wardens, Whitehaven.
Wt. 17oz. 6dwt."

There are four marks:—
(1) I.L. under a gem ring, for John
Langlands. There is a pellet between the
letters.
(2) Lion passant.
(3) Leopard's head crowned.
(4) Three Towers for Newcastle.

4.—A Silver Flagon with spout, but without a lid. Height, 4½ inches ; diameter at
the top, 5¼ inches. This is a very heavy
bold vessel quite unsuitable for the
Eucharistic Service. The marks are:—
(1) Leopard's head crowned.
(2) Three Towers.
(3) Lion passant.
(4) F, being the Newcastle date letter for
1772-3.
(5) I.C. under a vase, in a shaped shield,
for James Crawford Inscription : "Given
for the use of Trinity Chapel, Whitehaven,
by Joseph Glaister, merchant, 1773."

5.—Two modern silver cups. Marks :—
(1) S. H. over D. C.
(2) Lion passant.
(3) Leopard's head.
(4) Antique letter A.
(5) Queen's head, profile to the left.
They are of London make of the year
1856.

The Font was placed in the Church in
memory of the wife of Canon Dalton,
and bears upon a brass these words:—
"This Font is the gift of the relatives of
Mary, the wife of Canon Dalton, Vicar, in
affectionate remembrance of her interest
in the young of the parish. Born, March
2, 1815. Died, February 6, 1874."

The Brass Ewer of the Font was given
June 15, 1904, in memory of Hannah
Dickinson.

CHAPTER VI.

We now pass to the Churchyard.
Many of the old stones have been defaced
or lost. But some I am able to recover by
the transcript which I have already quoted
in connection with St. Nicholas, and from
other sources. One of the most interesting
is this :—

"Here lies interred the body of Mr.
Matthias Read, painter, who died November ye 8th, 1747, aged 78 years. Here also
lies Mrs. Elizabeth Read, his wife, who
died April ye 2nd, 1748, in ye 79th year of
her age."

Particulars of the life of Mathias Read
were given in the account of the Church of

St. Nicholas. The baptism of three of his
children is also given in the abstracts from
the Register of the same Church. The
death of two of these three children are
also on record : Jane died "March, ye 28,
17**," and William died, having just
passed his majority, August 7, 1724.

"Sacred to the memory of Daniel (le)
Fleming, of Rydal Hall, in the County of
Westmorland, who died 14th day of August,
1751, aged 31 years."

"Mr. John Hamilton, merchant, died
ye 10th of April, 1759, aged 70 years.
Faith Hamilton, his wife, November 15,
1755, aged 84 years.
Dorothy Hamilton, their grand-daughter,
died July 25, 1845, aged 93 years."

"Mr. Isaac Hamilton, surgeon, died
March 11, 1780, aged 71.
Mr. Francis Hamilton died July 11th,
1792, aged 76.
Isaac, his son, died on the coast of
Africa, in the year, 1765, aged 24.
Thomas, his son, died at Petersburgh, in
Virginia, November 13, 1759, aged 16.
Faith, his daughter, died November 1,
1745, aged 5 months.
John Hamilton, Esq., died May, the 15th,
1814, aged 74 years.
Lieut.-Col. Anthony Hamilton, of the
Honorable East India Company's Service,
died June, the 25th, 1830, aged 78."

(The Hamilton family was one of the first
to whom land was alienated, in Whitehaven,
by the Lowthers, after they obtained the
Lordship of St. Bees. Other names were
Littledale, Nicholson, Bardy, and Gale).

"In memory of Mr. Joseph Littledale,
merchant, who died October 22, 1774.
Joseph, his son ; Mary, his wife, Joseph,
their son ; Anthony, their son."

"In memory of Mr. Isaac Langton, mer-
chant, died May 17, 1740, aged 55 years.
Mrs. Frances Langton, died January 22,
1767, aged 83.
Mr. Robert Langton died in Mocha, aged
20.
Elizabeth Langton died August 12th, 1715,
aged 4.
Mr. Anthony Langton, merchant, died
March 3rd, 1746, aged 28.
Mrs. Ann Langton died October 3, 1792,
aged 71."

"Sacred to the memory of Thomas, the
son of Robert and Martha Jefferson, who
departed this life, 2 January, 1770, aged 21
years. Three infant children lying near
him."

"Mr. Robert Jefferson departed this life 18 October, 1779. aged 75 years. Martha, his widow, departed this life, 6 January, 1785, aged 59 years.

Robert, their son. died at New York, in January, 1783, aged 31 years.

Mary, their daughter, departed this life, the 17 April, 1787, aged 25 years."

"Near this place are interred Walter Lutwidge, Esq., and Elizabeth, his wife, with ten of their twelve children, and two of their grandchildren, James and Elizabeth Arbuckle."

"Mr. John Hudson, sen., died December 27, 1742, aged 75.

Mrs. Frances Hudson, his widow, died January 15, 1785, aged 93.

Mr. John Hudson, jun., died July 1, 1741, aged 24 years.

And three sisters lye here."

Mr. Thomas Hudson died September 30, 1806, aged 76 years.

Mrs. Frances Hudson, his widow, died October 4, 1817, aged 82.

John, son of Thomas and Frances Hudson died March 31, 1816, aged 54 years."

"Edward Carr Knubley, attorney-at-law, died 18th June, 1850, aged 64 years.

Edward, his son, died 6th October, 1841, aged 21 years.

Ponsonby, Martha, and Simon, his children, died in their infancy."

"Edwin Holwell Heywood, attorney, died 8th January, 1851, aged 68."

There are two very interesting and related stones on the east wall of the Church. They read:—

1.—"In memory of Anne, the beloved wife of Wilson Fisher, who departed this life on the 6th of October, 1836, aged 58 years.

And the said Wilson Fisher who died on the 7th October, 1844, aged 69 years."

[Thomas Fisher, of Whitehaven, married Mary Wilson, April 13, 1766. He died January 21, 1810.

His son, Wilson Fisher, was baptised December 10, 1774. He married Anne, daughter of Daniel Brocklebank, of Whitehaven, April 15, 1812.

His son, Thomas Fisher, was born November 24, 1814. He married June 4, 1844, Anne, daughter of Joseph Robinson, of Bolton Hall, Cumberland. He assumed by Royal licence (December 5, 1845) the surname and arms of Brocklebank, in lieu of Fisher. He was created Baronet by Letters Patent, July 22, 1885.—Sir Thomas Brocklebank, Bart. He died in 1906.]

2.—"In memory of Daniel Brocklebank, shipbuilder, who departed this life, March 7th, 1801, aged 59 years.

Anne, his wife, died March 7th, 1825, aged 85 years.

Daniel, the son of Daniel and Anne Brocklebank, died at Montego Bay in Jamaica, on the 20th of July, 1798, aged 25 years.

Sarah, their daughter, died the 15th of March, 1855, aged 82 years."

[The Brocklebanks were shipbuilders, originally, in New York when it was an English colony. On the declaration of war (1775), which resulted in the independence of the United States, the whole family came back to the old country and commenced ship building in Whitehaven. They were also renowned rope makers, especially before steel ropes came into use in the mines. Their rope walk was, at one time, at Corkickle. Among the seamen and others a "Corkickle" meant the best rope that could be got anywhere.]

CHAPTER VII.

We now pass to the Registers.

MARRIAGES.

1725, August 12. Mr. Peter Blaiklock and Ann Oulshaw.

1746, October 30, Robert Jefferson and Martha Skelton, both of Whitehaven. [Robert Jefferson was baptised in the parish of Aikton, January 19th, 1703-4. He was buried on October 21, 1779. The "Cumberland Pacquet" (October, 1779) has the following:—"Tuesday last, in Marlborough Street, in an advanced age, Mr. Robert Jefferson, many years a captain in a ship in the Virginia trade, and much respected as an honest man." One of his grandsons (Robert) bought "Springfield," Bigrigg, and another (Henry) built "Rothersyke," Egremont. A transcript of the tombstone of Robert and Martha Jefferson, which used to stand in Holy Trinity Churchyard, has already been quoted.]

1750, September 22: Isaac Keksick and Frances Littledale.

1752, April 24. Robert Wilkinson of Preston Hows, and Sarah Pearson, widow, of Whitehaven.

1772, February 27, Joseph Louis Desvillers Durrand and Sarah Kerton, by licence.

1788, May 2, Rev. James Piercy, Clerk, M.A., of the parish of St. Bees, and Bridget Peile, widow, by licence. In the presence of Margaret Spedding and Samuel Martin.

1791, July 21, Thomas Barwise, Fredericksbury, Virginia, and Mary Fisher. By licence. In presence of Betty Fisher and Eliz. Peile.

[Reference has been made to the Gilpin family several times in course of the chapters on St. Nicholas. The name appears both among the Baptisms and Burials.

At Holy Trinity we become still more intimate with the name. I will therefore give a few facts about four generations of this family:

1. Richard Gilpin, whose descent is traced back to Richard de Gylpyn, of the time of King John (1206), was baptised at Kendal, October 23, 1525. He studied physic, and was known as Dr. Gilpin. He became Rector of Greystoke, at the time of the Presbyterian regime, but retired at the Restoration (1660) though the Bishopric of Carlisle was offered to him. He bought Scaleby Castle and lived there, but afterwards became preacher to a dissenting congregation at Newcastle, where he died, February 16, 1699-70.

He had thirteen children, the eldest being William.

2. William Gilpin was born at Gray-stoke, while his father was Rector there. September 5, 1657. He became Recorder of Carlisle. In Whitehaven he managed the affairs of Sir John Lowther, and came into conflict with the Gales, especially Ebenezer Gale.

He died at Scaleby, August 14, 1724.

He had, in all, eleven children, though some predeceased him.

William, the third son, is of special interest to us.

3. This second William was born at Whitehaven, January 20, 1697-8. His baptism appears in St. Nicholas' Register on February 4th, of that year. He was a prosperous merchant, but died a young man, and was buried at St. Nicholas, March 21, 1735-6. He married Margaret, the second daughter of George Langstaffe, who was buried at Holy Trinity, December 24th, 1761. As a widow she married the Rev. W. Brisco, Rector of Distington, and Vicar of Holy Trinity, whom she also outlived; Mr. Brisco being buried January 25, 1744-5. This William Gilpin had one son and three daughters. His son also bore the name William.

4. William, this son was baptised at St. Bees, June 10, 1724, and was buried at St. Nicholas', Whitehaven, December 7, 1772. His wife was Betty, the daughter of Robert Hodgson, of Whitehaven. They were married at Holy Trinity Church, January 29, 1758.

They had seven sons and four daughters. They were all baptised at Holy Trinity, as is shewn in the above list.]

1801, January 19. Born 17th July, 1800, Henry, son of Henry Jefferson, merchant. [Henry, the father, was baptised in 1750. He married Ann, the daughter of Robert Tweedie, in Antigua, on May 18, 1780, and returned to Whitehaven. He died at his house in Cross Street, aged 77, in 1827 (Vide "The Pacquet.") The death of Ann, his wife, is recorded in the "Whitehaven Gazette," May 22, 1820: "On Friday last, in Lowther Street, Ann, the wife of Henry Jefferson, Esq., aged 57 years." The notice concludes with a note of high appreciation. Henry, the son (baptised 19th January, 1801), built Rothersyke, which was inherited by his son Robert, who died unmarried. Rothersyke was sold to Lord Leconfield.

There was an elder son (Robert), who is not named in this register. He married Elizabeth Brown. For some time he lived at Keekle Grove, but afterwards bought Springfield. He died Sunday, September 24, 1848. The son of Robert (Henry), married Mary Harris, daughter of Joseph Harris, of Greysouthen.]

1803, December 29 (born September, 1801), Margaret, d. of Henry Jefferson, merchant.

1803, December 29 (born August 2, 1802), Thomas, s. of Henry Jefferson, merchant.

1806, March 7 (born February 25), Charlotte, d. of Henry Jefferson, merchant.

1822, February 4, Mary Ann, d. of Thomas and Mary Ann Bridget Harrison (clerk).

1824, February 12, Eliza, d. of Thomas and Mary Ann Bridget Harrison (clerk).

1827, January 13, Sarah, d. of Thomas and Mary Ann Bridget Harrison (clerk).

1827, January 13, Sarah, d. of Thomas and Mary Ann Bridget Harrison (clerk).

1825, December 7, Dorothy, d. of Edward Carr and Mary Knubley.

[Dorothy was married as Dorothy Anne, vide *Cumberland Pacquet*, November 5, 1863.]

1826, January 22, Miles Ponsonby, s. of Edward Carr and Mary Knubley.

[Miles Ponsonby Knubley married 30th May, 1849, Anne, d. of Robert Jefferson, of Springfield, and died Rector of Plumbland. His son, the Rev. Edward Ponsonby Knubley, is Rector of Steeple Ashton, in Wilts.]

[Dorothy, named above, married Major Spencer. The other children of Edward Carr Knubley were:—

1. Edward, who died unmarried.

2. Catherine, who married Dr. John Bateman Wilson.

3. Ellen, who married Charles Fisher, of Distington Hall.]

1720, July 14, Elizabeth, d. of John and Eleanor Younger.

1758, December 4th, George Patrickson, of Newhouse.

1759, April 6th, Anne, d. of Mrs. Aerey.

1759, January 31st, Elizabeth Grayson, widow.

1762, June 24th, Sarah Aerey, widow.

1762, July 11th, Isaac, s. of Darcy Curwen.

1762, September 28th, Anne, d. of Mr. John Grayson.

1764, January 10th, Nathaniel Nicholson.

1764, March 1st, Mary, d. of Mr. Edward Fitzgerald, died of smallpox after inoculation.

1764, May 1st, Richard Sherwen, aged 86 years.

1766, September 6th, Mr. William Ponsonby.

1769, March 4th, died 1st, Elizabeth, wife of Mr. John Ranking, excise officer.

1767, September 22nd, Mr. James Wennington.

1771, March 4th, Mr. John Nicholson, Farmer.

1772, October 17th, Mrs. Mary Nicholson, widow.

1775, January 8th, John Grayson, malster.

1776, November 2nd, The Rev. Thomas "James," rector of Egremont. [This is a blunder for Jameson.]

1800, October 8th, Mrs. Frances Jameson, widow of the Rev. Thomas Jameson, formerly rector of Egremont.

1780, November 14th, Catherine Benson, widow, aged 97.

1782, June 2nd, Elizabeth, wife of Mr. John Ponsonby (died 31st May) aged 44.

1782, December 21st, Mr. John Ranking, officer of Excise, died 18th, aged 58 years.

1783, March 23rd, Mr. John Ponsonby, attorney at Law, died 21st March, aged 45.

1783, October 5th, Margaret, wife of John Benson, died ye 3rd, aged 73.

1784, May 29th, Mary Patrickson, of Wath, aged 39.

1785, April 13th, Isabella, d. of Thomas Patrickson, of the Isle of Man, aged 9 months.

1785, June 12th, Mary, wife of Mr. William Benson, attorney at Law, aged 25.

1786, March 9th, Edward Fitzgerald, surgeon, aged 59 years.

1787, July 15th, Anthony Smith, aged 67.

1788, April 12th, Mr. William Gaitskell, mercer.

1789, June 8th, died 6th, John Benson, died at Cockermouth, aged 71.

1790, March 22nd, Mary Grayson, widow, aged 70.

1792, September 25th, Thomas Grayson, of Yeorton, in the parish of St. John's, aged 78.

1793, January 16th, Sarah, wife of Darcy Curwen, of Gosforth, 88.]

1793, September 1st, Mrs. Jaine Grayson, of Crofside, widow, 72.

1796, August 25th, The Rev. Clement Watts, minister of Drigg and Irton.

1797, November 25th, Darcy Curwen, of Threepthwaite, in the parish of Arlecdon, aged 94.

1799, February 2nd, Mr. John Gaitskell, Surgeon, aged 37 years.

1799, September 8th, Margaret, wife of John Westray, Farmer.

1800, February 19th, Mr. Isaac Grayson, of Crofside, aged 55.

1805, December 8th, Capt. John Curwen, of Picket How, Bachelor, aged 67.

1807, July 25th, Thomas Benson, of Cockermouth, Esq., aged 65, died 21st.

1806, March 16th, died 14th, Robert Patrickson, Bachelor, aged 73.

Patrickson, of Whitehaven, widow, aged 70.

1803, January 29th, died 27th, Matilda

1768, February 7th, to May 16th. Twelve persons died of smallpox, one after inoculation.

1769, September 13th, William Benson, Farmer.

1781, November 18th, Mr. Robert Nicholson, Mercer, died 15th, aged 30.

1781, November 30th, Mr. John Nicholson, Farmer, died 28th, aged 56.

1807, March 22nd, John Benson, dyer, died 19th, aged 82.

1812, August 16th, Mr. Robert Nicholson, Bachelor, died 14th, aged 29.

CHAPTER IX.

Bigrigg.

In 1880 a district Church was erected at Bigrigg to accommodate the outlying portions of the Egremont parish, as they extend toward the parish of Hensingham, viz., Bigrigg, Moor Row, and Skailgill. The structure is substantial, commodious, and pleasing in many ways, but it has been built without any regard to orientation. The chancel lies to the North. The Church contains two good picture windows—one in the chancel, over the Holy Table, and the other above the Font, at the porch end.

The Font window was first erected not long after the dedication of the Church. It bears the words :—

"In piam memoriam paternam Maria Watts Jefferson hanc fenestram ponendam curavit."

These words are to be read :—

"Maria Watts Jefferson caused this window to be placed here, in dutiful memory of her parents."

The father of Maria W. Jefferson was Mr. James Gordon, of Dumfries. Her mother was Mary Brocklehurst, d. of Ralph Brocklehurst, of Hazel Holme.

On the picture portion are the words of Holy Scripture:—

"Suffer little children to come unto me, for of such is the Kingdom of Heaven." appropriate words, as the window directly overlooks the Font.

The Chancel window as placed in the Church ten years later. It bears this inscription:—

"In honour of Christ crucified, and in loving memory of Henry Jefferson, of Springfield, who died November 27th. 1895, aged 73 years, this window was dedicated."

There is a tablet on the wall of the nave, nearly opposite the entrance, in memory of a young private soldier who died in South Africa:—

"He fought for King and Country.
Pte.   2nd V. B.
7499   B. R.

In Memory of
William Henry Richardson,
Born June 19th, 1881; died while on active service in Johannesburg, South Africa, December 12th, 1901.
'Faithful unto death.'
Erected by public subscription."

The names of the Curates-in-Charge:—
The Rev. W. J. Wood.
  ,,   G. I. Tuck.
  ,,   A. Mence.
  ,,   W. Taylor (now of Cleator Moor).
  ,,   H. S. Moore.
  ,,   R. Woodward.
  ,,   J. Wharton.
  ,,   J. Ashworth.
  ,,   W. Fryar.

FRIZINGTON.

THE CHURCH OF ST. PAUL.

CHAPTER I.

THE BUILDING OF THE CHURCH.

In the matter of years, Frizington Parish is the infant among the parishes of Whitehaven Deanery. As a separate parish it is only five years old, though the Church building was erected nearly half a century ago. Frizington, like the surrounding district, is rich in Hæmatite and Coal, and the large influx of miners, consequent on the energetic and successful development of these resources, increased the population from 270 persons in 1851 to about 5,000 in 1868.

When the Rev. Richard Taylor (now the Rev. Canon Taylor, of Bromfield Vicarage, Carlisle) was appointed Vicar of Arlecdon, in 1861, he found only the Parish Church, with accommodation for little more than two hundred worshippers, and a small and inconvenient Schoolroom, in which to conduct Divine worship in Frizington. The urgent spiritual requirements of the growing population led him to project the Frizington Church scheme, which met with the hearty co-operation of the parishioners and the principal employers of labour in the district. At a meeting of the inhabitants of Frizington, and others interested in the welfare of the locality, held at Frizington Schoolroom, in October, 1862, it was unanimously resolved "that considering the large population of the township, and the likelihood of it increasing for years to come, and considering also that the Parish Church of the district is situated at a great distance from the most populous parts thereof, it is desirable that strenuous efforts should be made for building and endowing a Church at Frizington." An influential committee was formed to collect subscriptions, and otherwise to carry into effect the objects of the meeting, Thomas Dixon, Esq., of Rheda, being appointed treasurer, and the Rev. Richard Taylor and John Musgrave, Esq., of Whitehaven, secretaries. In July, 1864, matters had so far progressed that the foundation stone of the new Church was laid by T. Dixon, Esq., of Rheda. The building was opened for public worship February 17th, 1867, under a licence from the Bishop of the Diocese. But it was not consecrated till April 1st, 1868. The Church is built of red sandstone, from Crosslaken Quarry, and is roofed with bright Buttermere slates. All the exterior and

PART COPY OF THE INDENTURE

PURCHASE OF YEAMANS
ESTATE BY JEFFERSON
FAMILY IN 1832

This Indenture of four parts made the Twenty Eighth day of May in the Year of our Lord One thousand Eight hundred and thirty two –
Between Sir John Ogilvy of Inverquharity in the County of Forfar – in that part of the United Kingdom of Great Britain and Ireland called 'Scotland' Baronet - Eldest Son and Heir.......of Sir William Ogilvy late of Inverquharity aforesaid deceased of the first part - **Dame Sarah Ogilvy** of Inverquharity aforesaid - Widow of the said Sir William Ogilvy, **Hope Stuart** of Ballochere in the County of Perth in that part of the said United Kingdom called 'Scotland' Esquire **Donald Ogilvy** of Clorn in the said County of Forfar Esquire commonly called the Honourable Donald Ogilvy and Honourable Ogilvy of Cheltenham ~ in the County of Gloucester Esquire..........and Executor named and appointed by the said Sir William Ogilvy of the second part - **Walter Ogilvy** a Captain in His Majesty's Sixty Ninth Regiment - William Ogilvy James Balfour Ogilvy – and David Ogilvy of...... in the East

Indies Esquire – Thomas Ogilvy of Bombay in
the East Indies Esquire. George Keith Ogilvy a
Midshipman in His Majesty's Royal Navy –
Charlotte Ogilvy of the City of Edinburgh
Spinster and Alexander Charles Ogilvy now a
Student at the University of Glasgow being the
youngest Children of the said Sir William
Ogilvy – of the third part **and Robert Jefferson**
and **Henry Jefferson** of Whitehaven in the
County of Cumberland in that part of the United
Kingdom called England. Merchants - of the
fourth part – **Whereas** the said Sir William
Ogilvy at the date of **Trust disposition and
Settlement ....**
until her death................**Or**.........Lands,
Tenements and..........in the Island of Antigua
.................unreadable...........executed a
Trust Directive in Settlement - ....date on or
about the Seventeenth day of April One thousand
Eight hundred and thirty two attested by Law –
required **and** thereby gave granted .....conveyed
........unreadable.........**Sarah Ogilvy,
Alexander Ogilvy, Hope Stuart, Donald Ogilvy**
.... - sundry lands and
Heritages........unreadable............ the whole
Estate Heritable and moveable Real and
Personal.......determination
....
....
....
and so on...

Book J Indenture 1831 - 1834

This Indenture of four parts made the Twenty eighth day of May in this Year of our Lord One thousand Eight hundred and thirty two **Between** Sir John Ogilvy of Inverquharity in the County of Forfar in that part of the United Kingdom of Great Britain and Ireland called Scotland Baronet Eldest Son and Heir at Law of Sir William Ogilvy late of Inverquharity aforesaid deceased of the first part Dame Sarah Ogilvy of Inverquharity aforesaid Widow of the said Sir William Ogilvy, Hope Stewart of Balladan in the County of Perth in that part of the said United Kingdom called Scotland, Donald Ogilvy of Clova in the said County of Forfar Esquire commonly called the Honorable Donald Ogilvy and Alexander Ogilvy of Cheltenham on the Twenty of Gloucester Esquire Surviving Trustees and Executors named and appointed by the same Sir William Ogilvy of the second part Walter Ogilvy a Captain in His Majesty's Sixty Sixth Regiment, William Ogilvy, James Balfour Ogilvy and David Ogilvy of Bengal in the East Indies Esquire, Thomas Ogilvy of Bombay in the East Indies Esquire, George Frederick Ogilvy a Midshipman in His Majesty's Royal Navy, Charlotte Ogilvy of the City of Edinburgh Spinster and Alexander Charles Ogilvy now a Student at the University of Glasgow being the Younger Children of the same Sir William Ogilvy of the third part And Robert Jefferson and Henry Jefferson of Dalbeara in the County of Cumberland or that part of the said United Kingdom called England, Merchants of the fourth part Whereas the said Sir William Ogilvy being at the date of the Trust disposition and Settlement hereinafter mentioned and thenceforward until his death seized and possessed of or otherwise well entitled to the Messuages Lands Tenements and Hereditaments in the Island of Antigua hereinafter mentioned and intended to be hereby released or otherwise assured Made and duly signed and Executed a Trust Disposition and Settlement bearing date on or about the Seventeenth day of April One thousand eight hundred and twenty two Attested as by Law required And thereby Gave granted assigned conveyed and disponed to his Wife the same Dame Sarah Ogilvy herein Alexander Ogilvy Hope Stewart and Donald Ogilvy All and sundry Lands and Heritages Debts Heritable and moveable and in general His whole Estate Heritable and moveable Real and Personal of whatever nature or denomination and without any exception Unless as therein specially excepted whether situate in Scotland or furth thereof than belonging to him or which should belong to him at the time of his decease Real security but without any prejudice whatever to the aforesaid generality, All and whole his Messuages Lands Tenements and Hereditaments situate in the Island of Antigua in the West Indies including his Estates or plantations of York and New Division situate in the said Island with the Negroes and whole stock and effects which might be upon his said plantations and estates with full power to his said Trustees to sell and dispose of his whole Estate Heritable and moveable Real and Personal or such parts thereof as should be necessary for Answering the purposes herein after mentioned (excepting only his plate Linen Furniture Books Pictures Wines and Liquors which were to remain Unsold) either by Public Roup or private bargain and to grant Conveyances thereof binding his Heirs and Representatives in absolute Warrandice And to receive the prices thereof thereby discharging Purchasers from any responsibility respecting the Application of the same. And the same Testator appointed his same Trustees to be Executors of his same Will. And Whereas the same Testator departed this Life on or about the twenty ninth day of September One thousand eight hundred and twenty three without having revoked or altered the aforesaid Disposition of his Property except so far as the same are altered by an Instrument between in the said Testator Trust Deed but which do not affect the premises intended to be hereby granted and Conveyed And the same were duly Recorded in the Books of Council and Session in Scotland on the Eleventh day of October One thousand eight hundred and twenty three. And Whereas the same Surviving Trustees and executors of the same Sir William Ogilvy deceased have disposed of all the moveable and personal Estate of the said Testator (except such part thereof as the same Testator directed to remain Unsold) and in order to discharge the Legacies or Sums of Money bequeathed or charged as aforesaid And for payment of other sums of money pursuant to the Trusts of the same Testator Trust Deed and Settlement have Borrowed and taken up at Interest of Messrs Herringham and Lindsay of Edinburgh the Sum of Six hundred and fifty pounds Sterling of Patrick Maxwell Stewart of the City of London Merchant the sum of One thousand and five hundred Pounds Sterling from Mr Gray Robert Jefferson and Henry Jefferson the Sum of One thousand three Hundred and fifty pounds And in order to discharge the said two several sums of Six hundred and fifty pounds And One thousand five hundred pounds by the same Robert Jefferson and Henry Jefferson have Agreed to Advance and lend to the said Surviving

EXTRACT FROM BOOK OF
INDENTURE

SALE OF YEAMANS ESTATE TO
WILLIAM GOODWIN IN 1881

Know all men by these Presents that we Henry Jefferson of Springfield near Whitehaven in the County of Cumberland Esquire ~ Robert Jefferson of Rothersyke near Whitehaven aforesaid Esquire ~''~ carrying on business together in copartnership at Whitehaven aforesaid as merchants under the style or firm of Robert & Henry Jefferson, Jane Jefferson of Rothersyke aforesaid spinster and Mary Watts Jefferson of Springfield aforesaid the wife of the said Henry Jefferson do hereby nominate constitute and appoint Sir Oliver Nugent of Millars (?) in the Island of Antigua ......our true and lawful Attorney for us and each of us and in our and each of our names to sign seal execute and deliver a certain ~''~ Indentures of Conveyance expressed to be made between us the said Henry Jefferson and Robert Jefferson carrying on business in copartnership as aforesdaid, of the first part me the said Henry Jefferson of the second part us the said Robert Jefferson and Jane Jefferson of the third part me the said Mary Watts Jefferson of the fourth

part and William Goodwin of   in the
Island of Antigua of the fifth part of all that
plantation or Estate called Yeamans situate
lying and being in the Division of Old North
Sound and Falmouth in the Island of Antigua
containing by estimation two hundred and ten
acres or thereabouts butted and bounded on the
North side with the Estate called Parry's and
the High Road to the South with the Estates
called Rock Hill and Bodkins (?) to the East
with the Estates called Duers and Delaps and to
the West with the Estate called Big Duers or
.........otherwise butted or Bounded lying and
being together with all houses outhouses
buildings tenements Mills boiling houses
.....houses still houses carts carriages mules
horses asses cattle plantation utensils and
implements and all manner of rights privileges
casements appendages and appurtenances
whatsoever to the said plantation or Estates
lands messuages ....hereditaments and
premises ~ respectively belonging or in anywise
appertaining and also for us and each of us and
in our and each of our names to appear before
the Registrar or other proper officer for the time
being of the said Island of Antigua to register
and record in conformity with the laws of the
said Island of Antigua the said conveyance and
also to acknowledge the same to be as and for
the acts and deeds of us and each of us And we
authorize and impower our said Attorney for us
and each of us and in our and each of our

*names or name to do all acts matters and things
necessary for registering and recording the said
Conveyance in manner aforesaid and rendering
the same effectual according to the laws and
customs of the Island of Antigua. In Witness
whereof we the said constituents have hereinto
set our hands and seals this Twenty seventh day
of January One thousand Eight hundred and
Eighty one.*

*Signed sealed and delivered
by the said Henry Jefferson
Robert Jefferson Jane Jefferson
and Mary Watts Jefferson in the
 presence of*

*Lewis T Helder
Solicitor
Whitehaven*

*P C ......?....
Tivoli
Whitehaven
Accountant*

Know all Men by these Presents that
us Henry Jefferson of Springfield near Whitehaven
in the county of Cumberland Esquire, Robert Jefferson
of Rothergkes near Whitehaven aforesaid Esquires
carrying on business together in copartnership at
Whitehaven aforesaid as merchants under the style or
firm of Robert & Henry Jefferson — Jane Jefferson
of Rothergkes aforesaid spinster and Mary Watts Jefferson
of Springfield aforesaid the wife of the said Henry
Jefferson do hereby nominate constitute and appoint
Sir Oliver Nugent of Willars in the Island of Antigua
Knight our and each of our true and lawful Attorney
for us and each of us and in our and each of our
names to sign seal execute and deliver a certain
Indenture of Conveyance Expressed to be made between us
the said Henry Jefferson and Robert Jefferson carrying
on business in copartnership as aforesaid) of the first
part us the said Henry & the allow'd part us the said Robert
Jefferson and Jane Jefferson of the third part me the
said Mary Watts of the fourth part and William Goodwin
of   in the Island of Antigua of
the fifth Part, of all that plantation or Estate called
Yeamans situate lying and being in the Division of
Old North Sound and Falmouth in the Island of
Antigua containing by estimation two hundred and
ten acres or thereabouts butted and bounded on the
North side with the Estate called Pauy's and the High
Road to the South with the Estates called Lock Hill and Delops
to the East with the Estates called Duers and Adlops and to
the West with the Estate called Big Duers or Howeves otherwise
butted or Bounded lying and being together with all
                                                    horses

houses outhouses buildings tenements Mills boiling houses
curing houses still houses carts carriages mules horses
asses cattle plantation utensils and implements and all
manner of rights privileges easements appendages and
appurtenances whatsoever to the said plantation or Estate
lands Messuages tenements hereditaments and premises
respectively belonging or in anywise appertaining and
also for us and each of us and in our and each of our
names to appear before the Registrar or other proper officer
for the time being of the said Island of Antigua to register
and record in conformity with the laws of the said
Island of Antigua the said conveyance and also to
acknowledge the same to be as and for the acts and
deeds of us and each of us And we authorize and em-
power our said Attorney for us and each of us and in our
and each of our names or name to do all acts matters and
things necessary for registering and recording the
said Conveyance in manner aforesaid and rendering
the same effectual according to the laws and customs
of the Island of Antigua In witness whereof we the
said constituents have hereunto set our hands and seals
this twenty seventh day of January one thousand eight
hundred and eighty one

Signed sealed and delivered   Henry Jefferson   (LS)
by the said Henry Jefferson
Robert Jefferson, Saul
Jefferson and Mary Hatt   Robert Jefferson   (LS)
Jefferson in the Presence
of   Saul Jefferson   (LS)
    Lewis T Holder
      Solicitor   Mary H Jefferson   (LS)
      Whitehaven
P C Tripney
  Clerk
    Whitehaven
    Accountant

THE JEFFERSON FAMILY TREE

APPENDIX 'O'

Landowners at Aikton, near Wigton, Cumberland prior to 1696

Robert : (1)(the Founder
of the Dynasty

Born 1704
Baptised in the Parish of Aikton
on 19th January 1703(-4?)
Died 18th October 1779
Buried on 21st October 1779
at Holy Trinity Church, Whitehaven
Profession: Master Mariner and
Captain of a Ship in the Virginia Trade.
Residence: Marlborough Street,
Whitehaven.
Married: Martha Skelton of Whitehaven
in Holy Trinity Church, Whitehaven, in 1746
(Martha: Died 6th January 1783).
Robert buried at Holy Trinity Churchyard,
Whitehaven.

Father of:
Thomas (B: 1749: D: 2nd January 1770) (buried in Holy Trinity Churchyard)
Henry (1) (Second Son) **(B: 1750: D: 1827)** - See Below
Robert   (B: 1752: D: January 1783 in New York)
Sarah*   (B: 1754)
John   (B: 1757: D: at 9 mths)
Daniel   (B: 1758: D: at 4 wks)
Mary   (B: 1759: D: 1762)
Mary   (B: 1764: D: 17th April 1787)

*baptised as the daughter of Robert & Martha (Holy Trinity Register) but is not
mentioned on other family trees. There is some doubt as to whether she was part of
the Jefferson family as there were other families by name of Jefferson living in
Whitehaven at the time.) Sarah married William Bacon, a Mariner, in Holy Trinity
Church in 1780.

Henry (1)
(The Founder of the Firm)

Born 1750   Died 13th December 1827
Baptised in the same year.
Profession: Master Mariner.
Master of the vessel '*Gale*', 200 tons, in 1775,
trading with Virginia. He started the family
business and embarked on Trade in the West
Indies directly connected with this new
business of Wine and Spirits Merchants.
Residence: 4 Cross Street, Whitehaven.

Married: Ann(e) Tweedie (B: c 1766)
daughter of Robert Tweedie of Antigua, on
18th May 1780, in Antigua, and later returned
to Whitehaven.
Henry died at his home in Cross Street and
was interred at Holy Trinity Churchyard,
Whitehaven.
Ann(e) died (at a Lowther Street address) on
20$^{th.}$ or 22nd May 1820

Father of:
Anne (B: 1782: D: 1820)
Jane (B: 1782: D: 1821) (Married Joseph Robinson, Surgeon)
Robert (2)(B: 1785: D: 1848) - See Below
Sarah (B: 1787: D: 1787)
Mary (???) (Married 1831?)
Harriet (B: 1791: D: 1792)
Sarah (B: 1791: D: ???)
Elizabeth (B: 1793: D: 1826)
Eleanor (B: 1795: D:???)
Catherine (B: 1797: D: ???)
Charlotte (B: 25th February 1800: D: 7th March 1806)
Henry (2)(B: 1800: D: 1877) - See Below** (Married Ann Davidson (D: 1854) in
1824)
Margaret (B: September 1801: D: 1828)
Thomas (B: 2nd August 1802 (3?): D: 1836 in Valparaiso)

Robert (2)   **Born 1785 in Antigua(?) Died on Sunday 24th**
September 1848
Occupation: Wine Merchants and Importers.
Residence: Keekle Grove, Whitehaven,
then purchased Springfield, Bigrigg, in 1841,
on the death of John Ponsonby,
Married: Elizabeth Brown (D: 1851)
Robert was buried at St Michael's and St.
Mary's Church, Egremont

Father of:
Mary (B: 1821: D: ???)
Henry (3) ((B: 1823: D: 1896) - See Below
William (B: 1824: D: 1824)
Ann(e) (B: 1827: D: ?? (Married Miles Ponsonby Knubley on 30th May 1849)
Miles Knubley became Rector of Plumbland
Robert (4) (B: 1828: D: 1868)(Married Catherine Stephenson)
Elizabeth (B: 1832: D: ???)(Married John Edward Weston)
William (B: 1832: D: 1833 at 6 mths)

Henry (2)   **Born 17th July 1800   Died 19th July 1877**

Baptised at Holy Trinity Church,
Whitehaven on 19th January 1801.
Occupation: Wine Merchants and Importers
Residence: Hensingham House, Whitehaven;
then built Rothersyke, later inherited by his
son Robert (3) and subsequently sold to Lord
Leconfield.
Married: Ann Davidson (D: 1854) in 1824

Father of:
Robert (3)(B: 1826: D: 1902) *Did not marry.*
Henry Thomas (B: 1827: D: 1874) (Married Mary Smith in ?   One ?Child **Henry**)
Charles (B: 1829: D: 1852)
Mary Ann (B: 1830: D: ???)   (Married John Harris of Greysouthen)
William (B: ??? : D: ???)
Catherine (B: ??? : D: ???)   (Married W. Harrison of Winscales)
Frank (B: ??? : D : ???)
Jane (B: 1835: D: ???)
Harriet (B: 1837: D: 1877)   (Married a Mr Tetley of Liverpool)

**Note: Robert (2) and Henry (2) gave their names to the family
business of Robert & Henry Jefferson, Wine Merchants**

Henry (3)   Born 16/08/1823   Died 27 /11/1896
                                       Baptised at Holy Trinity Church,
                                       Whitehaven
                                       Residence: Springfield, Bigrigg
                                       Henry Married (1) in 1856:
                                       Mary, the Second Daughter of Joseph Harris
                                       of Greysouthen
                                       (Died: 1861)
                                       They had Four Children: Robert (5), Hugh ,
                                       Mary & Elizabeth
                                       (2) in 1864 Mary (Maria) Watts Gordon, the
                                       Daughter of James Gordon of Dumfries.
                                       Mary's Mother was Mary Brocklehurst,
                                       daughter of Ralph Brocklehurst of Hazel
                                       Holme, near Wath Brow.
                                       They had Two Children: Henry & Gordon
                                       Henry was buried at.....................

By First Marriage Father of:
Robert (5), of Rosehill)(B: 1857: D: 1942) - See Below (Married Constance Lumb
(Lamb?) daughter of Mr Lumb (Lamb?), Homewood, Whitehaven, in 1894)
Mary Cowperthwaite (B: 1858: D: 1920) (Married Joseph Dickinson: b: 1846:
                                       d: 1909)

190

Joseph Hugh (B: 1859: D: 1920) (Married Elizabeth Ann Dixon in 1888)
> **Father of:**
> **Mary (B: 1889:** (Married: Capt. T.W.
> McDonald in 1914)**: D: 1919)**
> **Rheda Kathleen (B: 1890** (Married
> Capt.Robert N. Gordon in 1911) **D: ???)**
> Capt. Gordon Killed in Action in 1914)

Elizabeth (B: ???: D: 1923)

By Second Marriage Father of:
Henry Watts (B: 1865: D: 1902)
Gordon (B: 1868: D: 1915)

NOTE: **Robert (2)** (D: 1848) was the Elder brother of: **Henry,
(2)(D:1877)** J.P., of Rothersyke, the Father of **Robert (3)(D:
1902)** of Rothersyke – therefore **Robert (3)** was the cousin of
Henry (3) of Springfield

Henry (3)(D: 27/11/1896) carried on business in partnership with
his Uncle, **Henry (2)**, J.P., of Rothersyke, until the latter's death
in 1877. **Henry (3's)** cousin **Robert (3)**, of Rothersyke, joined
Henry in the business in the year **Henry (2)** died.

Henry (3) (Died 27/11/1896) retired from the family business
some years prior to 1896 and his son **Robert (5)**, of Rosehill, took
his place. When **Robert (3)**, of Rothersyke, retired in 1896,
Hugh, brother of **Robert (5)** joined his brother ; the business
once again being controlled by two brothers.

ROBERT (5)

Born: 1857	Died 1942
Residence:	Springfield, Bigrigg
Married:	Constance Lumb (Lamb?)
in 1894	

Robert is buried in Egremont Churchyard

Father of:

Henry (4)(B: 1896:   (Married Grace Mackie Crichton in 1946)
          D: 1ˢᵗ June 1979)   (Grace died at Annan on 1ˢᵗ August 1974)
(Headstone in Egremont Cemetery)   **Father of:**
                              Constance Elizabeth
                              Elizabeth Drennan
Constance: (B: 1897)
Robert (B: 1900)   (Married Elizabeth Wadham in 1927)

Author's Note:

The above Family Tree is provisional only and is subject to alteration and correction. Some difficulty has been experienced by the Author as it was the custom, in earlier days, of retaining the same Christian names through succeeding generations. The Jefferson family was no exception to this custom and the names *Henry* and *Robert* occur frequently and sometimes confusingly. Added to this there are occasional discrepancies in, or omission of, dates and in some cases the records indicate individual births in one family being recorded as born in the same year. Also, some birth and death dates are contradicted in various Church and other records.

Brian Parnaby

E.& O.E.

MAP SHOWING SUGAR ESTATES LOCATED ON ANTIGUA
(With Inventory of successive Owners from 1750 to 1921)

YEAMANS ESTATE

Date: 1878

Owners: R & H Jefferson

According to the Copies of the Indentures made available by the Director, National Archives, Government of Antigua & Barbuda, the Jefferson's purchased this Estate in 1832 and sold it in 1881.

In the History of the Island there is mention, on several occasions, of the name 'John Jefferson'* and 'John Jeaffreson' (*vide Estate no. 100 – 'Jeffersons/Sion Hill), the owner in 1750 being one 'John Jefferson'. It is not possible that this owner is the 'John Jeaffreson', brief details of whom appear hereunder, because of the dates involved. However, in those days where alternative spellings of names and places were common-place, it is likely that this John Jefferson was a descendant of 'John Jeaffreson'. There would be few people on a small Island such as Antigua sharing the same (or a similar) name who would not be related.

However, it is improbable that the Cumbrian Jefferson's and the Jeaffreson's were related. John Jeaffreson was a 'Suffolk' man. He is recorded in the Island's records as being the Commander of a Ship, the 'Hopewell' in 1624. Robert Jefferson was, of course, born at Aikton near Wigton, in 1704, eighty years after Jeaffreson was in command of the Hopewell.

Likewise, there is no mention in the Cumbrian Jefferson family history of any connection with the island of Antigua any earlier than in the late Eighteenth century, from 1775 onwards when Robert (1) and Henry (1) sailed the 'Gale' to Antigua, on which Island Henry (1) married Ann(e) Tweedie in 1780.

A 'Persons' search of the Museum of Antigua and Barbuda for the 'Yeamans' Estate and the 'Jefferson's' discloses in some details names, occurrences and dates relating to the estate. Some of the information is obviously inaccurate, for example: it is recorded that, in 1780/05 Captain Robert Jefferson married Anne Tweedie in Antigua. His SON, Henry, married Ann(e) as mentioned above.

There has been a plethora of information regarding the Cumbria Jefferson's connection with estates on Antigua and some of it cannot be confirmed because of contradictory dates, etc. Also, data regarding the 'other' Jefferson/Jeaffreson is confusing in places.

Book I, 'The History of the Island of Antigua', by (Dr.) Vere Langford Oliver, MRCS, ENG, LRCP, provides some interesting background information on Yeamans and Jeaffreson.

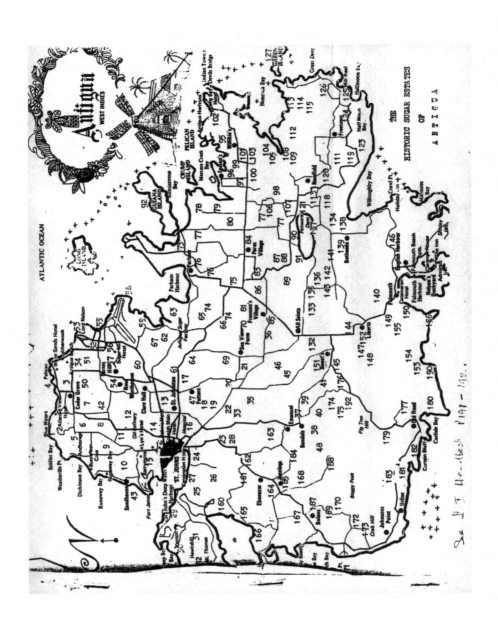

196

ST. PETER'S PARISH

Estate	Owners in....Early years	1752	1760	1820	1821	1829	1821	1921
73. CREWS *		Val Morris	Val Morris	James Conll	Dr J. Conll		C.C. Tudway	C.C. Tudway
74. CEDAR HILL *		Hon Edw. Byan	Edw. Byan	Wm. Dynn			Chas. Berkeley	C.C. Tudway
75. VERNON'S		Slingby Bethell	J.J.J. Vernon	Major Vernon		Vernon	Ers James Barkley	Ers Jas. Barkley J.J. Carr
76. PARRY'S & FARMS	PARRY, Clent, Tudway 1659	Chas. Tudway	Clement Tudway	John P. Tudway	Robt. C. Tudway		C.C. Tudway	C.C. Tudway
77. ESTES HOPE & **	LUCAS/CRAWFORDS Charles T.,Clent, T.	Sir Wm. Codrington's Sir Charlington						
	BETES HOPE & ** Jean Ball,1668 C.							
	COTTON, GLEBE * Godrington,1669 CO II							
78. COCOA NUT MILL *			Codrington	Sir B. Clring'n	Sir C. B. Codrington		Sir G.W.K. Codrington	Sir G. Codrington
79. DAVES *		Geo. Crump	Davis & Edwards					
80. KERGIE'S CREEK *		Sam & Wm. Hibbs	James Hibbs	J.D. Edwards	Ers Edwards		V.L. Codrington	Desous, Jardine Deacons/T'd
81. GILBERT'S *		Francis Farley	Ers Farley					
82. FREEMAN'S, Upper		Natl Gilbert	Rev. N. Gilbert	Ers Thos. Rogers	Ers Thos. Rogers		V.L. Parker & Co	John P. Post V.D. Bastia
83. COCHRAN'S, Lower		Arthur Freeman		Rev. N. Gilbert Dr. N. Gilbert	Dr. N. Gilbert		J. & R. Berkeley Ers R. Berkeley G. Berkeley
84. PARES		Archd. Cochran		Rev. N. Freeman H.W. Freeman	H.W. Freeman			
85. JONAS *		John Pare		Indigo Thomas Indigo Thomas	Indigo Thomas		V.L. Parker Co	
86. SANDERSON'S *		Jonas Langford		Saml. Otto-Bayer Saml. Otto-Bayer	Owen Fell		Wm. E.H. Fell	V.O.S. Poll J.R. Der etc.
87. OSBORNE'S		Ers Saul. Vickham	Jonas L'ford Brook P.L. Brook	Thos. Brook		J.W.L. Brook	A.J. Branch	
88. PARRY'S		Geo. Crump	Jas. Gordon Jas. Gordon	Jas. L. Gordon		V.L. Martin	Jas. Barkley	J.W.L.Barkley
89. BIG DEER'S		Hamilton Kirby	Dr Thos. Fairbanl.					
90. LIL LE DEER'S *		Ron John Duer	Saul. Martin Ers V. Martin	Col T.F. Brown		Messrs G.Ottley	Geo. Mcindrew	R. Bryson
91. TOWNAHS *		Ret yet begun	Geo V. Kirby Ers L. Kirby	G.L. Ottley		Thos D. Foote	Thos D. Foote	R. Bryson
X92. GUANA ISLAND *		Shoot Tucnan	Roland Kirby Ers John Duer	Kennimy & Anderton V.L. Parker Co		Ers Geo Goodwin		Ers Geo Goodwi
		Ron El Byan	John Duer Ers John Duer	William Lee			Ers. Goodwin	
			Drinton & Hig	J. Wood & Benmett		H.B. Jefferson	Wm. Goodwin	Geo. Goodwin E

SIR   CODRINGTON

G. W. K. CODRINGTON

ST. PHILIP'S PARISH

Estate	Owners in....Early years	1752	1760	1820	1821	1829	1921
95. ROCHS *		Sir Wm. Codrington C'topher Bethell	Sir L.Codrington	Dr L.M. Osborne		V.H. Edwards	Ers Rev Drinkwater L.Pentima
96. PARSON MAULES *		Saml. Laricourt	John D. Halliday	Geo. V. Ledeatt	Geo. V. Ledeatt		Edward Fecliett	L.Deacons A. Edwards
97. GLANVILLE'S *		Chas. Dunbar		Ada V. Tollemache	Ada J. Tollemache		Lord Combermere	14 C.Mrs Goodwin G.Farkley
98. COLLINS		Nicholas Collins	John Ledeatt	Geo. V. Ledeatt	Geo. V. Ledeatt		Wm. Goodwin	Wm. Goodwin R.J.D. Goodwin
100. GIANT'S		Ers of Carr	Jas. Grant	O. Poll	O. Poll		Edw. Beckett	Deacons
101. JEFFERSON/SION HILL *		John Jefferson	John Taylor				Ers E.M. Fell	V.O. S. Poll J.T. Dew etc
102. BEEBE/BEDLLFORD		John Kayers	John Kayers	John D. Taylor				
103. COMFORT HILL *		Robt. Maliten	T. Montgomery	John J. Valier	O. Poll		D.W. Scarville	Wm. Goodwin R.S.D. Goodwin
104. GRAY'S, BELFAST *		Walter Sydney	Thomas	Thos B. Edwards	O. Poll		James Barkley	J.T. Der etc
105. VICKEM'S *		John King	Ron John Gray	J.Gray & Wm Gilchrist	Ers Walter Edwards		D.C. Olum	Ers Wm Goodwin
106. ELLIOTT'S *		Jos & Saml Vian	Ron Nathan Kayer	Jos. Martin	Ers Gilchrist		L.S. Anthonyson	C'mers & Barkley R Cotton
107. DELAPS & LONG LANE *		Ers Saml. Elliott	Saml. Elliott	John Laricount	J. Martin		Ers French	Villian Goodwin F.J. Goodwin
108. GILMOR'S *		Ron Benjn. King	John Elliott	Sir Geo Colebrook	Ers of French		Jas. Barkley	C.L. Thomas
109. KIRKS *		Miss Mary Gayrer	John Laricourt	Ers Nickolas Symes	Ers Laricourt		V. Goodwin	Lord Combermere
110. GOBLE		Thos. King	Sir Geo Colebrook	Messrs Rydana	Ers of Wood		V. *	
	John Richardson	Martha Goble	Ledeall & Scott	Ers Wm. Karman	Lyne			
	1705 John Goble.		John Lynch		Ers Wm. Karman			

APPENDIX 'Q'

COPY OF CONVEYANCING
DOCUMENT BETWEEN
HENRY JEFFERSON and
GEORGE WILLIAM BENNETT:

1876

(Property on Island of Antigua)

*To all to whom these presents shall come I
Henry* Jefferson of Rothersyke in the County
of Cumberland Esquire send Greeting.
Whereas by an Indenture of Conveyance
bearing date the Nineteenth day of August One
thousand Eight hundred and forty four and
made between Joseph Leaver Bindon Esquire
therein described as the acting Provost Marshal
of the Island of Antigua of the first part and
Robert** Jefferson since deceased and myself
the said Henry Jefferson both therein described
as of Whitehaven Merchants trading under the
firm of Robert and Henry Jefferson of the other
part.
After reciting as therein was recited It was
intended that for the considerations therein
mentioned the said Joseph Leaver Bindon in his
capacity of Acting Provost Marshal of the said
island ....and confirm unto the
said Robert Jefferson since deceased and myself
our heirs and assigns all that piece or parcel of*

*land with the Messuage or Dwelling house
outhouses wharf stores and all other tenements
and buildings thereon situate lying and being in
the City of Saint John in the said island butted
and bounded on the North by Wapping Street in
the said City of Saint John to the South by the
Sea or Harbour of Saint John to the East by
lands there of Mrs Bennett and to the West by
lands there of Mrs Fanny ......To hold the same
with the appurtenances unto the said Robert
Jefferson since deceased and myself our heirs
and assigns. To the use of us the said Robert
Jefferson since deceased and myself our heirs
and assigns in as full ample perfect and
beneficial a manner to all intents and purposes
As the said Joseph Leaver Bindon in his
capacity of Acting Provost Marshal of the said
island lawfully could or might grant and convey
the said Messuage Tenement hereditaments and
premises with the appurtenances. And whereas
the said Robert Jefferson died on the twenty
fourth day of September One thousand Eight
hundred and forty eight leaving me the said
Henry Jefferson him surviving. And whereas I
the said Henry Jefferson have lately sold the
premises comprised in the above recited
Indenture to George William Bennett for the
price or sum of Two hundred and fifty pounds
and in order to carry out the said sale I have
determined to appoint Sir Oliver Nugent of the
said Island of Antigua Knight and his son
Oliver Nugent the younger to be my Attorneys*

*and Attorney for me and in my name to execute
all proper deeds and assurances and do all acts
matters and things which may be necessary for
that purpose.   Now know ye that I the said
Henry Jefferson for divers good causes and
considerations ………….. moving as by these
presents make …….nominate constitute and
appoint the said Sir Oliver Nugent and his son
the said Oliver Nugent the younger and each of
them to be my true and lawful Attorneys and
Attorney for me and in my name and on my
behalf and as my act and deed to sign seal
execute and deliver any deed or deeds
Instrument or Instruments in writing which
may be necessary or expedient for granting and
assuring the said premises unto the said George
William Bennett or as he shall direct or appoint.
And generally for me and in my behalf to do
perform and execute all or any such other acts
deeds assurances matters and things as shall be
necessary or expedient in and about the
premises for the purpose of carrying out the
said sale and as fully and effectivally (sic) to all
intents and purposes as I myself could or might
do if personally present. And I do hereby
expressly declare and argue that the receipt and
receipts which shall be given by my said
Attorneys or Attorney or either of them for all or
any part of the purchase money of the said
premises shall be a good and sufficient
discharge or good and sufficient discharge*

to the purchase or purchasers thereof for all or so much and such part of such purchase money as shall be in such receipt or receipts respectively expressed or acknowledged to be received and that the said purchaser or purchasers shall not afterwards be bound to see to the application of the same monies nor be responsible for the loss, misapplication or nonapplication thereof or any part thereof. And I do hereby fully authorize my said Attorneys and Attorney to retain and deduct out of the said purchase monies all costs charges and expenses which they or he shall sustain and incur in the execution of the power or trust hereby reposed in them. And I do hereby argue to ratify and confirm all and whatsoever my said Attorneys or Attorney or either of them shall lawfully do or cause to be done by virtue of these pursuits. And lastly I do hereby declare that all payments which shall be made to my said Attorneys or Attorney or either of them by any person or persons before he or they shall have notice of my death or revocation of the authority hereby given shall be valid and official to all intents and purposes and shall be binding on my heirs Executors and Administrators notwithstanding my death or revocation of such authority before such payment shall be made to my said Attorneys or Attorney.

In witness whereof I the said Henry Jefferson have hereunto set my hand and seal this

fifteenth day of May One thousand Eight
hundred and Seventy Six.
Signed sealed and delivered)
By the before named Henry)
Jefferson in the presence of

Thos. H Brockbank
    Solicitor
       Whitehaven

F.W. Kirkbride
    Clerk
       Whitehaven

*   **Henry (2)**
** **Robert (2)**

To all to whom these presents shall come I Henry
Jefferson of Rothersyke in the County of Cumberland
Esquire send Greeting Whereas by an Indenture of Conveyance
bearing date the Nineteenth day of August one
thousand eight hundred and forty four and
made between Joseph Leaver Bindon Esquire therein
described as the acting Provost Marshal of the Island
of Antigua of the one part and Robert Jefferson since
deceased and myself the said Henry Jefferson both
therein described as of whitehaven Merchants trading
under the firm of Robert and Henry Jefferson of the other
part After reciting as therein was recited It was witnessed
that for the considerations therein mentioned the said
Joseph Leaver Bindon in his capacity of acting Provost
Marshal of the said Island did grant bargain sell
alien enfeoff and confirm unto the said Robert Jefferson
since deceased and myself our heirs and assigns all
that piece or parcel of land with the Messuage or
Dwelling house outhouses wharf lines and all other
tenements and buildings thereon situate lying and
being in the City of Saint John in the said Island
butted and bounded on the North by Wapping Street
in the said City of Saint John to the South by the Sea
or Harbour of Saint John to the East by lands then
of Mrs Bennett and to the West by lands then of Miss
Fanny Wootten To hold the same with the appurtenances
unto the said Robert Jefferson since deceased and myself
our heirs and assigns to the use of us the said Robert
Jefferson since deceased and myself our heirs and assigns
in as full ample perfect and beneficial a manner
to all intents and purposes as the said Joseph Leaver
Bindon in his capacity of acting Provost Marshal of the
said Island lawfully could or might grant and convey
the said Messuage tenement hereditaments and premises
with the appurtenances And whereas the said Robert Jefferson

died on the twenty fourth day of September one thousand
Eight hundred and forty eight leaving me the said Henry
Jefferson him surviving And whereas I the said Henry Jefferson
have lately sold the premises comprised in the above recited
Indenture to George William Bennett for the price or sum of
two hundred and fifty pounds and in order to carry out
the said sale I have determined to appoint Sir Oliver Nugent
of the said Island of Antigua Knight and his son Oliver
Nugent the younger to be my attorneys and attorney for me
and in my name to execute all proper deeds and assurances
and do all acts matters and things which may be necessary
for that purpose Now know ye that I the said Henry
Jefferson for divers good causes and considerations me
thereunto moving do by these presents make ordain
nominate constitute and appoint the said Sir Oliver Nugent
and his son the said Oliver Nugent the younger and each of
them to be my true and lawful attorneys and attorney for me
and in my name and on my behalf and as my act and
deed to sign seal execute and deliver any deed or deeds
Instrument or Instruments in writing which may be necessary
or expedient for granting and assuring the said premises
unto the said George William Bennett or as he shall direct
or appoint And generally for me and in my behalf to do
perform and execute all or any such other acts deeds
assurances matters and things as shall be necessary
or expedient in and about the premises for the purpose of
carrying out the said sale and as fully and effectually
to all intents and purposes as I myself could or might do
if personally present And I do hereby expressly declare and
agree that the receipt and receipts which shall be given by my
said attorneys or attorney or either of them for all or any part
of the purchase money of the said premises shall be a good
and sufficient discharge or good and sufficient discharges to
the purchaser or purchasers thereof for all or so much and such
part of such purchase money as shall be in such receipt or
receipts respectively acknowledged to be received And
that the said purchaser or purchasers shall not afterwards be
bound to see to the application of the same monies nor be
responsible for the loss misapplication or nonapplication thereof
or any part thereof And I do hereby fully authorize my
said attorneys and attorney to retain and deduct out of the
said purchase monies all costs charges and expenses which
they or he shall sustain or incur in the execution of the power
or trust hereby reposed in them And I do hereby agree to
ratify and confirm all and whatsoever my said attorneys or
attorney or either of them shall lawfully do or cause to be done
by virtue of these presents And lastly I do hereby declare
that all payments which shall be made to my said attorneys

204

or Attorney or either of them by any person or persons before he she or they shall have notice of my death or revocation of the authority hereby given shall be valid and effectual to all intents and purposes and shall be binding on my heirs executors and Administrators notwithstanding any death or revocation of such authority before such payment shall be made to my said Attorney or Attorneys.

In witness whereof I the said Henry Jefferson have hereunto set my hand and seal this fifteenth day of May one thousand Eight hundred and seventy six

Signed sealed and delivered }
by the before named Henry }   Henry Jefferson   (JS)
Jefferson in the presence of }

     Jno Jos H Brockbank
       Solicitor
        Whitehaven

F.W. Kirkbride
   Clerk
   Whitehaven.

THE JEFFERSON'S

of

WHITEHAVEN

ILLUSTRATIONS

19. *The Famous 'Fine Old Rum' Label.*
20. *Various photographs of the interior of.*
    Jefferson's Office, as it was at the
to *closure of the business in 1998.*
    Complete with family portraits (courtesy
25. *of 'The Rum Story').*
26. *Ordnance Survey map of 'Springfield'.*
27. *Ordnance Survey map of 'Rothersyke'.*
28. *Illustration of a Marlborough Street*
    Dwelling (c 1761); (similar to home of   Robert (1) Jefferson).
29. *Cutting from Whitehaven News*
    14th. April 1932: Court case heard by
    Robert (5) Jefferson.
30. *Jefferson's advertisement;*
    Whitehaven News; 7th. June 1979.

Attachment: Result of search by Museum
                of Antigua & Barbuda for the 'Yeaman' Estate. Only available through that
                Museum's database.

THE LATE ROBERT JEFFERSON, ESQ., J.P., D.L.,
OF ROTHERSYKE.
From a Photograph by Mr. A. Wilson, Whitehaven.)

Robert (3) Jefferson, J.P., D.L., of Rothersyke (1826-1902).

1

Portrait of Robert (5) Jefferson, J.P.C.A. (1857-1942).

COCKERMOUTH.

BURIAL BOARD.—Chairman: Rev. W
Members: R. F. Brown. J. Walker. R
Dixon. R. Robinson. W. Elliott. J. Mum
Peacock. H. Fawcett. Josiah Hall. Ce
Burn. Curator: J. D. Kirkbride

PROVIDED SCHOOLS.—Chairman: W
ander. Vice-chairman: J. Straughan.
Rev. W. E. Dixon. H. Fisher, J. R. Blea
A. Sutton. and J. Robertson. M.D.

POLITICAL.—Cockermouth Conservat
Secretary: J. H. Drummond. Cockerm
sion Liberal Unionist Association: Se
H. Fawcett. Mountain View. Cockerm
kermouth. Liberal Unionist Association
A. Birkenshaw. Challoner-street. Co
Liberal Club: Secretary, J. Dallas.
Liberal Association: Secretary, Mrs. J.
son. Brigham. Primrose League: Secre
Senhouse. The Fitz.

FRIENDLY SOCIETIES.—Loyal Cocke
Oddfellows: Secretary. W. T. M'M
Helens-street. Rechabites: Secretary
Anderson. the Bridge: superintendent
Tent. Mr. William Clark. New-str
Abstinence Sick and Burial Society:
Mr. D. Pennington. Belle Vue. Forest
jary. Mr. Jos. Armstrong. Main-street.

FOOTBALL.—Cockermouth Northern I
Secretary. J. Farnell. Low Sand Lan
mouth. Crusaders Association Club:
F. Kemp. Belle Vue.

CRICKET CLUB.—Secretary. W. H. S
street. Treasurer: J. W. Watson. Ct
trict Bank.

HUNTING.—Cockermouth Hunt (Beag
H. Peacock. Cumberland (West) F
Master. J. H. Jefferson. Cumberland Ott
Master: J. H. Jefferson.

PUBLIC HALLS.—Public Hall. Sta
seating capacity. 1,000: lessee. I. Ba
Hotel. Drill Hall. St. Helens-street. se
city. 1,800; Sergt. M'Ghie. Royal
Rooms. Crown-street. seating capacity
Wm. M'Clellan. Royal Hotel. in Ct
Freemasons' Hall. Main-street. seating
400; proprietor. Mr. J. Cannon. A
Hotel. Main-street. Court House. Cock
seating capacity. 200.

LAWN TENNIS CLUB.—Secretary. J
Elvira House.

GOLF CLUB.—Secretary, E. H. Wil
street.

PHOTOGRAPHIC CLUB.—Secretary,
Mavo-street.

WORDSWORTH INSTITUTE. — Secr
Hall. Elmhurst.

DISTINGTON.

PARISH COUNCIL.—Chairman: Rev.
Hodgson; vice-chairman. Mr. J. Rope
lork: Rev. L. G. W. Lumb. Dr. Castles.
son-Walker, J.P., W. Wilson. T. Garre
an. J. Seeds. T. Bell. J. Timmins.
Edward Plaskett. J. Kerr. and J. Robi
W. Birkett, clerk. Meetings every thr

SCHOOL MANAGERS.—Chairman: Re
Hodgson: Dr. Castles. Messrs. J. Rope
kett. W. Wilson. Rev. L. G. W. Lumb, i
M'Meckan; with Mr. W. Birkett, corr
and H. Hill, attendance officer. Meeting

J. H. JEFFERSON, ESQ., J.P., M.F.H.,
CUMBERLAND FOXHOUNDS (WEST).
(From a Photograph by Mr. H. Mayson, Keswick.)

ST. MARY'S LEAGUE OF THE CROSS INSTITUTE.
—Duke-street:—President: Rev. R. E. Kershaw.
Secretary: J. E. Byrne. Treasurer: Robt.
Woolaghan.

HOCKEY AND TENNIS CLUB.—President: Dr.
Clarke. Joint Secretaries: G. Walmsley. J. Bell.
and Miss Coulthard.

CONSERVATIVE ASSOCIATION.—President: Mr.
J. Stirling. Secretary: Mr. Robert Lowery, Mon-
treal-street. Lindow Habitation Primrose League.
—Ruling Councillor: Mrs. J. R. Bain, Bolton Hall.
Gosforth. Secretary: Mr. J. J. Robinson.

LIBERAL ASSOCIATION.—President: Mr. David
Ainsworth. The Flosh. Cleator. Rooms secretary:
Mr. D. Smith. Queen-street, Cleator Moor. Trea-
surer: Jas. Dalziel Liberal Club.

FRIENDLY SOCIETIES.—Loyal Providence Lodge
of Mechanics. secretary. James M'Dowell. Wath
Brow. Loyal Ehen Lodge of Mechanics. secre-
tary: Wm. Fisher. Trumpet Road. Hematite
Lodge of Oddfellows. secretary. Samuel Tembey.
Irish National Foresters, secretary: J. Woods.
Duke-street.

Joseph Hugh (Hugh) Jefferson M.F.H. (1859-1920).

3

LIEUT. R. JEFFERSON,
COMMANDING WHITEHAVEN TROOP, W.C.Y.C.
(From a Photograph by Mr. A. Wilson, Whitehaven.)

LIEUT. J. H. JEFFERSON,
ATTACHED TO WHITEHAVEN TROOP, W.C.Y.C.
(From a Photograph.)

WESTMORLAND & CUMBERLAND YEOMANRY.

THE FORMATION OF A TROOP AT WHITEHAVEN.

The formation of a troop of the W. & C. Yeomanry Cavalry for Whitehaven and the West Cumberland district has been a rapid and complete success, and the recruits are now assiduously engaged in preliminary drills in preparation for the approaching training. The W. & C. Yeomanry regiment was first enrolled in 1821, the grandfather of the present Earl of Lonsdale, Colonel H. C. Lowther, taking a principal part in raising the regiment and sparing neither effort nor necessary expense for that purpose. There were originally six troops, and these, as is usual, were named after the districts in which they were chiefly raised. These were Milnthorpe, Shap (which subsequently became the Lowther troop), Appleby, Dalemain, Kendal, and Edenhall. Following out the plan of localising the force, each of these troops was commanded by a gentleman of the neighbourhood in which it was raised, and as far as

possible similarly officered throughout. Nine years after the establishment of the regiment, on a revision of the yeomanry service, the number and strength of the regiments were reduced. Some were discontinued, and others had troops disbanded. This was the case of the W. and C. Yeomanry, which lost the Milnthorpe troop. Eleven years afterwards the place of the Westmorland troop was filled, on that occasion also by West Cumberland, the new troop being that of Wigton, which afterwards became the Carlisle troop. The recent disappearance of the Kendal troop was not unexpected, though one would have supposed that the Kendal district was a likely one to have maintained the strength and efficiency of its contingent. It is disbanded by a general order dated March 10th, as from the 1st March, and the enrolling of the new Whitehaven troop dates from March 12th. As we have noted from time to time there has been a most satisfactory supply of recruits and the troop will have, it is said, the finest average physique in the regiment, for out of the first batch of troopers measured for uniforms the tallest was 6ft. 4in., only one 5ft. 6in., and the average of 26 no less than 5ft. 11in.

The troop is commanded by Lieut. R. Jefferson, and his brother, Lieut. J. H. Jefferson, is attached to the troop. Lieut. R. Jefferson is the eldest son of Mr. Jefferson of Springfield, resides at Rosehill,

married the elder daughter of Mr. Lamb, of Homewood, and has a son born recently. Lieut. R. Jefferson has held a commission in the regiment for some ten years, and is in every way well fitted for the command now bestowed upon him. He is a magistrate for the county, and locally is known as a good sportsman. He is, and has been for some years master of the Whitehaven Harriers, and some few years ago was frequently seen in the saddle at steeplechase meetings in Cumberland and on the Border, where he had a fair share of success, his well-known mare, St. Bridget, being the best he ever had at the game.

Lieut. J. H. Jefferson, brother of the foregoing, and second son of Mr. Jefferson, lives at St. Helens, Cockermouth. He married the only daughter of the late Mr. Dixon, of Rheda, and has a family. Lieut. J. H. Jefferson is also a magistrate for the county, and has served a considerable time in the regiment. In early life Lieut. J. H. Jefferson spent some time ranching in Wyoming, and since his return he has occasionally ridden in local steeplechases, and a year or two ago won the Cumberland Foxhounds Point-to-Point race. He is secretary to the Cumberland Hunt and to the West Cumberland Otter Hounds, and whips in to his brother with the Whitehaven Harriers. He is a director of Messrs. Jennings Bros., Ltd., and a member of the Cockermouth District Council.

Lieutenants Robert (5) and Joseph Hugh Jefferson, WhitehavenTroop, Westmorland & Cumberland Yeomanry Cavalry (c. 1896?).

Photograph of 'Springfield' House (2005).

5

Photograph of 'Springfield' Lodge (2005).

6

Photograph of Rothersyke House (2005).

7

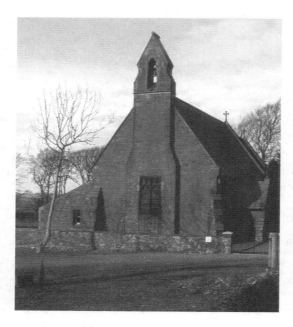

St. John's Church, Bigrigg (adjoining Springfield House) (2005).

8

Photograph taken from Oil Painting of the Brigantine 'British Queen'.

9

Illustration of Whitehaven Harbour, 1841.

10

Illustration of Whitehaven Harbour, 1850.

HOUND TRAILING PRESIDENT PASSES

His 50 Years' Public Service

MR. ROBERT JEFFERSON, J.P., C.A., one of the outstanding figures in the public life of West Cumberland during the past half century, died at his home at Springfield, Bigrigg, on Sunday. The news of his death came as a profound shock, as, in spite of his 84 years, he appeared to be in good health on Saturday morning. As recently as Thursday he presided at a meeting of the Whitehaven Area Committee of the Hound Trailing Association. A few hours previously he had attended a meeting of the Whitehaven Magistrates, to whom he tendered his resignation as chairman of the Probation Committee, but was prevailed upon to retain the office.

Descendant of a very old West Cumberland family, Mr. Jefferson was a son of the late Mr. Henry Jefferson, J.P., D.L., of Springfield, and was educated at Harrow.

Multifarious as were the activities of Mr. Jefferson, his long service as a Magistrate and his long presidency of the Hound Trailing Association were outstanding.

He was appointed a Magistrate in 1891 and for 19 years was deputy-chairman of the Whitehaven Bench. Twelve years ago he succeeded the late Mr. W. McGowan as chairman, an office he held until January last. Then, on his retirement, he was presented with a silver salver by his fellow-Magistrates. During his long service as a J.P., Mr. Jefferson administered the law with strict impartiality, but his sympathies were always with women and children. He was particularly severe with those found guilty of cruelty to animals or children, and with the perpetrators of mean crimes.

In 1904 Mr. Jefferson was elected a County Councillor for the Egremont (North) Division (now represented by his son, Henry) and continued to serve on that body until the day of his death. He was elected an Alderman in 1917. He was also a member of the Standing Joint Committee and served as a special constable.

Always interested in education and young people, he was elected chairman of the Egremont Group of Schools in 1904, was a former governor of St. Bees School, and for many years was a governor of the Whitehaven County Secondary School. These duties he carried out conscientiously, paying personal visits during school hours.

A warm supporter of hospital and district nursing activities Mr. Jefferson filled the office of president of the West Cumberland District Nursing Association and was one of the oldest trustees of the Whitehaven and West Cumberland Hospital. He was also a trustee of Whitehaven Savings Bank, his association with that institution dating from 1886.

TWO CHAMPION HOUNDS

In hound trailing matters it was often said that Mr. Jefferson was the H.T.A. Certainly no man has done so much for the sport, and he was unanimously re-elected president of the Association at every annual meeting since its inception 33 years ago. Not only was he the founder and only president, but he took a very active part in the affairs of the Association and was a fairly successful owner. One of the best hounds he ever owned was Climber, who won the H.T.A. championship in 1912. That honour did not come his way again until 1940, when the championship was carried off by Leader. Another great hound owned by him was Duleman, the winner of the first trails held at Springfield and first winner of Lord Leconfield's Cup in 1906.

Whilst hound trailing was for the last 40 years his chief sporting interest, Jefferson's more. St. Bridget's racing career ended in 1857, but from her Mr. Jefferson bred a gelding, Bakary, which added lustre to his dam's name by winning more than 20 races in the northern counties. Mr. Jefferson's own career as a rider ended while riding Beggar Boy at Carlisle. The horse stumbled and rolled on to his rider, inflicting injuries which necessitated his retirement from steeplechasing.

Hounds of any kind always held an interest for Mr. Jefferson and for many years he was master of the Whitehaven Harriers, a pack disbanded in 1901. He was an admirer and friend of Tommy Dobson, founder and master of the Eskdale Foxhounds, and presided at the presentation made to Tommy on his retirement in 1905.

IN THE YEOMANRY

Many old cavalry men still remember Mr. Jefferson as an officer in the Cumberland and Westmorland Yeomanry. He joined the regiment in 1885 and was the first commanding officer of the Whitehaven Troop, which he and his brother, Mr. Hugh Jefferson, raised in 1896. He retired from the Yeomanry in 1901 with the rank of honorary major.

Cricket, too, was a sport in which Mr. Jefferson took a keen interest. As a young man he played for the Gentlemen of Cumberland team and for more than 30 years was president of Egremont Cricket Club. For an even longer time he was president of the Egremont Recreation Club and presided at the opening ceremony of the club's pavilion in 1909.

For 64 years Mr. Jefferson was connected with the family business of wine and spirit merchants. This business was started in 1785 and has remained in the family unbroken through five generations. After five years in the firm's employ, during which he was their representative in London and Spain, Mr. Jefferson was taken into partnership and was head of the firm from 1896. The firm's business activities were spread all over the world and in addition to owning plantations in the West Indies the firm for many years owned its own ships. In 1924 Mr. Jefferson took into partnership his elder son, Henry, who of recent years has done most of the active business of the firm.

In 1894 Mr. Jefferson married Miss Constance Lumb, of Wray Castle, Westmorland, and Homewood, Whitehaven, and for many years they lived at Rosehill, Moresby. The death of his wife, in 1926, was a severe blow for Mr. Jefferson, and it was the memory of his own happy married life that made him so sympathetic toward women and children who appeared before him as a Magistrate. Mr. Jefferson is survived by two sons, Mr. Henry Jefferson, Springfield, and Mr. Robert H. Jefferson, Gosforth, and a daughter, Mrs. Leonard Wilson, of Kirkby Lonsdale.

COURT TRIBUTES

At Whitehaven Court on Monday Mr. W. H. Wandless, who succeeded Mr. Jefferson as chairman of the Bench in January, paid a tribute to the memory of his predecessor. Mr. Jefferson, he said, was one of the outstanding figures of his generation. He had done great service for the county, especially as a Magistrate and County Councillor. Only the previous Thursday Mr. Jefferson had attended a meeting of the Probation Committee and had tendered his resignation as chairman. His fellow-Magistrates, however, had persuaded him to carry on.

Mr. O. F. Ormrod, clerk to the Magistrates, on behalf of himself, his clerk (Mr. Jackson), and the staff, also spoke in tribute to Mr. Jefferson and expressed sorrow at his passing.

Supt. W. S. Brown, on behalf of the

*Photograph and Obituary of Robert (5) Jefferson
(born 1857; died 1942).*

Photograph of Memorial Tablet in St Bees Priory:
Henry (2) Jefferson (1800-1877).

Photograph of Yeamans Estate Mansion Antigua (now a Ruin).

14

Yeaman's House (taken in the 1930s).

15

The Old Windmill on the Yeaman's Plantation.

16

Distant photograph of the Old Windmill.

17

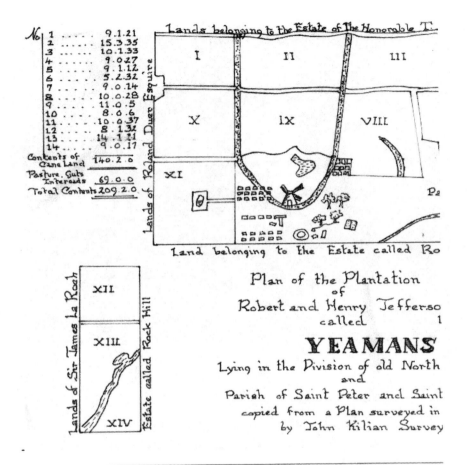

No		
1	.....	9.1.21
2	.....	15.3.35
3	.....	10.1.33
4	.....	9.0.27
5	.....	9.1.12
6	.....	5.2.32
7	.....	9.0.14
8	.....	10.0.28
9	.....	11.0.5
10	.....	8.0.6
11	.....	10.0.37
12	.....	8.1.31
13	.....	14.1.11
14	.....	9.0.17

Contents of Cane Land   140.2.0
Pasture. Guts. Interoads   69.0.0
Total Contents 209.2.0

Lands of Roland Duer Esquire

Lands belonging to the Estate of The Honorable T.

I   II   III

X   IX   VIII

XI   P2

Land belonging to the Estate called Ro

Lands of Sir James La Roah

Estate called Rock Hill

XII

XIII

XIV

Plan of the Plantation
of
Robert and Henry Jefferso
called   1

YEAMANS

Lying in the Division of old North
and
Parish of Saint Peter and Saint
copied from a Plan surveyed in
by John Kilian Survey

Plan of the (Yeaman's) Plantation of Robert & Henry Jefferson.

18

The Famous 'Fine Old Rum' Label.

19

Various photographs of the interior of Jefferson's Office, as it was at the closure of the business in 1998. Complete with family portraits (courtesy of 'The Rum Story').

20

21

22

23

24

25

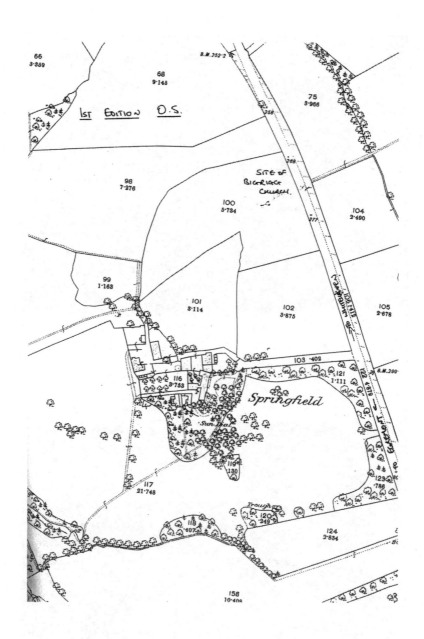

Ordnance Survey map of 'Springfield'.

26

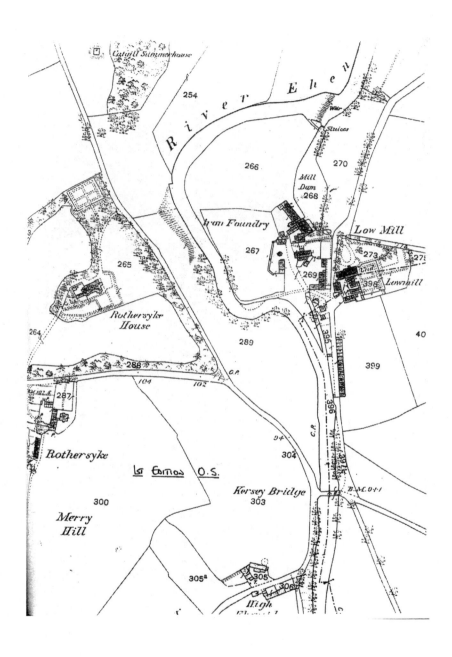

Ordnance Survey map of 'Rothersyke'.

In 1726 twenty yards of wharf was built on the seaward side of the Old Quay and in 1730 the lighthouse on the end of the Quay was repaired. Two years later the Trustees decided to repair and strengthen the Bulwark and work was commenced in September 1733. They also decided to build a second bulwark or tongue. This is the structure known variously at different times as the Merchants' Quay, the Old Tongue, the Sugar Tongue and Fish Quay. Originally it was to be sited where the Lime Tongue now stands but the position was altered in the planning stage. It was completed in 1735. In 1734 a breakwater was built between Tom Hurd's rock and the shore.

In 1739 it was agreed to build a mole 'behind the present Pier (i.e. the Old Quay) for the reception of a few of the largest ships when fully laden'. In 1742 John Reynolds submitted a plan for extending this quay (now known as the Old New Quay) by 100 feet at an estimated cost of £1,250. As the work was proceeding it was agreed to buttress the quay and to build a nine foot high parapet.

In 1750 it was resolved to build a new tongue out from the end of Marlborough Street. In contrast with the Merchants' Quay or the Old Tongue it became known as the New Tongue and later as the Lime Tongue. In 1767 the Trustees agree to add thirty yards to the Old New Quay, to shorten the Sugar Tongue by twenty yards, to lengthen the Old Quay by sixty yards and to move the lighthouse to the end.

The North Wall was started as a result of discussions held in 1766, more work was done on it following another resolution in 1780 and in 1785 it was agreed to add a return to the North Wall. This is the straight part of the Devil's Elbow, the additional portion being added in 1804.

In 1823 John Whidbey and Sir John Rennie were consulted about extending the limits of the harbour. This resulted in the plan for the West Pier which they suggested run N.N.W. from the western corner of the New Quay for 145 yards, then canting N.E. for 110 yards and again canting E.N.E. for a similar distance. A North Pier was visualised by them but it was not until 1833 that Rennie provided a detailed plan for this.

Work on the West Pier started towards the end of 1823 and continued until the end of 1830 when it had reached a point 340 yards from the New Quay. As the work progressed it was found that sand was accumu-

75

*Illustration of a Marlborough Street
Dwelling (c 1761); (similar to home of Robert (1) Jefferson).*

28

"LORRIES A NUISANCE

WHITEHAVEN CHAIRMAN AND NO REFLECTING MIRROR CASES

For failing to have a reflecting mirror on his car at South Street, Egremont, on March 22, John S. Moore (19), Irtside, Holmrook, was ordered to pay the costs (4s) at Whitehaven Court on Thursday. Defendant did not appear, but sent a letter pleading guilty.

Maurice Boyd (18), mechanic, Galloping Horse Inn, High Harrington, was fined for a similar offence at 9-10 p.m. He also sent a letter pleading guilty and was also ordered to pay the costs (4s). P.C. Laydon proved both cases.

The Chairman (Mr. R. Jefferson) remarked that Boyd's case was worse since he drove a lorry. "These motor lorries are a nuisance on the highway; they take up all the road and they make out they do not see anything behind them. They will now have to have reflectors and in the future when reported fines will be imposed."

---

fast was partaken of Mr. and Mrs. Taylo spend their honeymo at Distington.

COCKERMOUTH C INTO

On Friday an Crown Street, Cock head injuries to The a signalman on the riding a cycle when The driver of the car Whitehaven. Ridley conscious and remai for two hours. He Ellis and Dr. Abra home in Bowman's r is severely cut abou

THE MAGISTRA Court, on Thursday ferson (chairman), Flynn, P. H. Fox, son, J. McDonald, Rowe (Mayor).

Cutting from Whitehaven News 14th. April 1932:
Court case heard by Robert (5) Jefferson.

Jefferson's advertisement; Whitehaven News; 7th. June 1979.